What the Insurance Companies
DON'T Want You to Know About **YOUR RIGHTS**

THE INSIDER'S GUIDE TO NEW MEXICO AUTO ACCIDENT CLAIMS

WITH:

12 Dirty Tricks the Insurance Adjuster
Will Use to Wreck Your Claim

S. CLARK HARMONSON

WORD ASSOCIATION PUBLISHERS
www.wordassociation.com
1.800.827.7903

HARMONSON LAW FIRM
345 N. Water St., Ste. S-3
Las Cruces, NM 88001

915-584-8777
clark@clarkharmonsonattorney.com

www.clarkharmonsonattorney.com

ISBN: 978-1-63385-381-2

Designed and published by
Word Association Publishers

205 Fifth Avenue
Tarentum, Pennsylvania 15084
www.wordassociation.com
1.800.827.7903

TABLE OF CONTENTS

1. 9 COMMON MYTHS AND MISCONCEPTIONS ABOUT YOUR CAR ACCIDENT CLAIM. 17
2. SHADY AUTO INSURANCE COMPANY TACTICS. 21
3. TOP 5 WORST AUTO INSURANCE COMPANIES IN NEW MEXICO. 29
4. DO I NEED TO HIRE A LAWYER FOR MY CAR ACCIDENT? 35
5. HOW TO CHOOSE A QUALIFIED PERSONAL INJURY ATTORNEY. 45
6. WHAT YOU GET WHEN YOU HIRE AN EXPERIENCED CAR ACCIDENT LAWYER. 53
7. THE CAR ACCIDENT CLAIMS PROCESS. 57
8. TOP 5 CAR ACCIDENT QUESTIONS ANSWERED. 65
9. WHAT YOU SHOULD DO IMMEDIATELY AFTER AN ACCIDENT. 73
10. THE RULES OF THE ROAD: HOW WE HOLD NEGLIGEN DRIVERS ACCOUNTABLE FOR THEIR ACTIONS. 79
11. WHAT ARE THE MOST COMMON TYPES OF INJURIES IN A CAR ACCIDENT? 97
12. HIT AND RUNS, UNINSURED MOTORISTS AND UNDERINSURED MOTORISTS. 103
13. ACCIDENTS INVOLVING 18-WHEELERS – A DEADLY PROBLEM. 109
14. CAR ACCIDENTS CAUSED BY EMPLOYEES IN WORK VEHICLES. 113

15. WRONGFUL DEATH AND SURVIVAL CLAIMS. 119

16. WHAT TO DO IF YOU ARE INVOLVED IN AN ACCIDENT WITH A STATE, CITY OR COUNTY OWNED VEHICLE. 123

17. BICYCLE ACCIDENTS. 125

18. MOTORCYCLE ACCIDENTS. 129

19. REPAIRING OR REPLACING YOUR VEHICLE AFTER AN ACCIDENT. 133

20. HOSPITAL AND MEDICAL LIENS. 137

21. CASES WE DO NOT ACCEPT. 143

22. RESULTS. 147

23. WHAT OUR CLIENTS HAVE TO SAY ABOUT US. 151

24. ABOUT THE AUTHOR. 155

WE ARE DIFFERENT
WE ARE HERE FOR YOU

You have probably been bombarded daily by TV advertisements for car accident attorneys who promise the world. They promise to be tough, to be strong, to be aggressive. They show smiling actors pretending to be clients with wads of cash in their hands acting like they just won the New Mexico lottery. Unfortunately, these TV lawyers rarely live up to their promises. For starters, when people actually hire those firms, they rarely meet who they saw on TV. Instead, they are passed off to paralegals or less experienced lawyers and receive something much different than expected. Second, these TV personalities rarely, if ever, go to the courthouse to advocate for their clients. Instead, they run "personal injury mills" and settle cases as quickly as possible.

At Harmonson Law Firm, we are different. We help good people injured in bad accidents get the treatment and money they deserve. Most of our cases come from referrals from satisfied former clients, other lawyers and healthcare providers. We only select a limited number of cases every year so that we can give our clients the personalized service they deserve. We do not allow our paralegals to negotiate with the insurance company. Instead, a qualified personal injury attorney is in charge of every aspect of our clients' cases from the initial consultation through trial, if necessary. We are in the trenches of the local courthouses week in and week out fighting for our clients. More importantly though, we care about our clients. Yes, we are tough and aggressive when the case calls for it, but we actually put our clients' needs first. We know that meeting a lawyer is scary enough, and we work hard to treat our clients with compassion and respect. At every turn, we strive to make our clients feel at home so that as much stress is alleviated as possible.

Since 2004, Clark Harmonson has limited his practice exclusively to representing people who have been seriously injured in accidents and medical malpractice mishaps. We have had great success (as chronicled later in this book), and our mission at Harmonson Law Firm is to get our clients the most money possible for their car accident claims. Our New Mexico office is located in Las Cruces, New Mexico and we take cases throughout New Mexico. We will travel anywhere in New Mexico to meet with you in person if we both agree that our law firm is a good fit for your injury claim. Don't want to come into the office for a visit? We are available to handle most all of your case virtually and many of our clients never have to come into our office because of our investment in technology like electronic signature capture and videoconferencing.

FOREWORD:

THIS BOOK IS FOR **YOU**, THE CAR ACCIDENT VICTIM

Let me present you with a story:

I was driving to work on Interstate 25 in heavy traffic. Suddenly, the vehicle in front of me stopped. Luckily, I was paying attention and I also stopped in the rush hour traffic. When I looked in my rearview mirror, I saw that the pickup truck behind me was not paying attention to the flow of traffic. There was nothing I could do to get out of the way. I braced for impact and I heard a loud crash as the pickup truck rammed into me and pushed me forward. My airbag deployed and the next thing I remember is sitting in the car dazed and confused about what had just happened.

I immediately had a bad headache and pain was shooting up and down my spine. I was barely able to get out of the car. Everything was a blur. The next thing I remember is police sirens. They were not very nice to me as I was trying to gain my wits. They asked for my driver's license and insurance and went about their business. I looked for my cell phone to call my husband, but I couldn't find it in the aftermath of the wreck.

After around 30 minutes, an ambulance arrived. By this time, I was feeling dizzy and pain was racing throughout my body. I sat on the back of the ambulance as the EMTs performed an evaluation. They said that I should go to the hospital to get checked out. A witness at the scene of the crash was nice enough to help me call my husband and tell him to meet me at the hospital. The police gave me an incident card with the other driver's insurance information. They told me that the report would be ready in about 10 days. They didn't explain how I could get the report.

When I got to the hospital, they put me in a room separated by curtains. After a few hours, they performed a battery of tests on me and gave me some medicine. The ER doctor spent a few minutes with me and told me that I should go home, rest and call my regular doctor in the morning. The tests didn't show any broken bones or internal bleeding. My husband took me home and I slept all that night and couldn't get out of bed the next day because of the pain.

When the initial shock of the accident was over, we tried to figure out what to do next. The car was in an impound lot in the other part of town. We needed to get my computer out of the back of our car but didn't know what to do. We got a call from the pickup driver's insurance company and they wanted to take my recorded statement. The adjuster said that he was doing an investigation and that we should just give the statement to help things along. He was pushy with me and my husband and wouldn't answer all of our questions. When I asked if the insurance was going to pay my medical bills, I didn't get a straight answer. When I asked him about the car, the adjuster suggested that we should take the car to a body shop. He gave us the name of one he preferred. He said he wasn't able to give me a rental during his investigation. I didn't know if I should trust the adjuster or not.

When I saw my primary care doctor after the accident, she told me that I had suffered from whiplash. She said I should get some therapy. I didn't know if I should use my health insurance through work or whether the other driver's insurance should cover the medical bills. A few days after the accident, I got a bill from the hospital and was shocked to learn that it was several thousand dollars. They also sent us some legal paperwork that I didn't understand.

I haven't been able to work since the accident. My boss told me that I am not going to get paid while I am absent. I need the money that we make each week to help pay the bills; if I miss too much work, we will have a hard time making ends meet. I wasn't sure if the other driver's insurance was going to pay me while I missed work.

At this point, I thought maybe I needed to hire a lawyer to help me. I initially thought we could just handle it on our own, but now I am worried that I am making a mistake. I have never hired a lawyer before, and the thought of calling a lawyer's office makes me a little bit nervous. Would hiring a lawyer be too expensive? I don't have enough money to pay the lawyer up front. I don't know if I should hire one of the lawyers that I see on television commercials all of the time or whether I should try and find a lawyer some other way. Plus, I want to know how much I should expect to receive for my injuries in the accident. Can I recover my lost wages? Am I entitled to pain and suffering? Do we have to file a lawsuit? If so, I have never done that before.

If this story sounds familiar, you are not alone. Every week, thousands of people are involved in car accidents throughout New Mexico. You probably have many of the same worries and questions as those posed in this story. **The good news is that there is help.**

I wrote this book to help you cut through all of the confusion surrounding your car accident. I want you to have as much information as possible as you navigate the maze that happens after a car accident. I want you to have this information **BEFORE** you hire a lawyer and **BEFORE** you talk to the insurance adjuster and potentially wreck your injury claim. You have one chance to get this right. This book is your ultimate guide to making the right decisions when it comes to your car accident claim.

S. Clark Harmonson

DISCLAIMER:

THE INFORMATION IN THIS BOOK **IS NOT LEGAL ADVICE**

The State Bar of New Mexico requires that I inform you that the information in this book is for general information purposes only. Nothing in this book should be taken as legal advice for any individual case or situation. This book and its information are not intended to create, and receipt or viewing does not constitute, an attorney-client relationship. I am not your lawyer until we enter into a written agreement for me and my firm to be your lawyer.

I hope that the information in this book is useful to you in your dealings with the insurance company, in deciding whether or not you need to hire an attorney, and which attorney to choose once you make that decision. But, please do not interpret anything in this book as specific legal advice about the unique facts and circumstances surrounding your case. I can only give you quality legal advice once we have entered into a written agreement for me to be your lawyer.

With that said, let's talk about the car accident process in New Mexico.

CHAPTER: 1

9 COMMON MYTHS AND MISCONCEPTIONS ABOUT YOUR CAR ACCIDENT CLAIM

1. **The insurance company will be fair.** Whether you know it or not, you are at war with the insurance company and the insurance industry. From the minute you had your car accident, the insurance company for the at-fault driver began working hard to deny or minimize your claim. An insurance adjuster might pretend to be nice to you, but his or her **only goal** is to save their boss—the insurance company—money. Even if you send a reasonable settlement demand, don't expect the insurance company to give you a reasonable settlement offer in return.

2. **The insurance company will pay my medical bills promptly.** The insurance company is not obligated to and will not pay your medical bills as you submit them. The

insurance company will only pay you once you reach a settlement of all of your claims and have signed a release of their insured or after you have received a final, non-appealable court judgment against their insured.

3. **I am required to give a recorded or written statement to the insurance company.** There is no requirement that you must provide the insurance company for the at-fault driver any written or recorded statement. In fact, these statements can be extremely prejudicial to your case. We have settled countless car accident cases without having our clients give a recorded statement. When an adjuster asks me, my standard answer is always a firm "No," and yours should be too.

4. **I can sue the other driver's insurance company if they aren't being fair.** In New Mexico, you are generally not allowed to sue the at-fault driver's insurance company. In fact, at trial, the rules of evidence prevent you from ever mentioning the other driver's insurance. However, unlike some states like Texas, New Mexico allows the injured person to sue the other driver's insurance company if they engage in certain instances of bad faith under the Hovet doctrine (based on a New Mexico Supreme Court case decided in 2004).

5. **All lawyers are the same when it comes to injury cases.** Perhaps the most important decision you will make after your car accident will be the lawyer you choose to

help with your case. Yet, choosing the right lawyer can be extremely difficult. Every time I turn on a TV or drive down the interstate, I see the same type of ad promising easy cash and aggressive representation. They all say the same things. This book is written to help you see through the advertisements and find the right lawyer for your car accident case.

6. **Car accident laws are the same in every state.** Did you know that New Mexico has many favorable laws that protect car accident victims that are better than the laws of other states? For instance, in New Mexico, the at-fault driver's insurance company does not get the benefit if your own health insurance pays some or all of your medical bills. You are entitled to recover all of the billed medical bills even if your insurance company negotiates and pays a deep discount with your healthcare providers. Further, New Mexico has "pure comparative fault" rules which allow you to recover a percentage of your damages even if you are partially or even mostly at fault for causing the accident.

7. **Hiring a lawyer is too expensive.** A good personal injury lawyer can dramatically increase the value of the case. Don't just take my word for it. The results of a 2014 study from the Insurance Research Council (IRC) found that the decision to hire an attorney pays substantial dividends for automobile accident victims. In the report from the IRC titled "Attorney Involvement in Auto Injury

Claims," the IRC found that insurance payouts are, on average, 3.5 times higher for clients who have hired an attorney than for those without one.

8. **A jury will always be fair to me.** The insurance industry has paid millions and millions of dollars in spreading the myth that car accident victims are only out for money. As a result, and because of tort reform efforts, juries in New Mexico are not always generous in car accident cases. We always prepare every case as if it will go to trial, yet many times discretion is the better part of valor and a settlement before trial is in our client's best interests. I had a good trial lawyer tell me once, "It's not all candy canes and rainbows at the courthouse."

9. **I have to hire a lawyer no matter what.** One reason I wrote this book is to give you information to help you decide if you really need a lawyer. If your accident is minor and your injuries are also minor, you can probably handle your case on your own. I will give you details in this book that you can use to decide if you need a lawyer. If you make the decision to not hire a lawyer, there will be plenty of useful information in this book to help you deal with the insurance company on your own.

CHAPTER: 2

SHADY AUTO INSURANCE COMPANY **TACTICS**

Insurance companies have one goal—to create profit for their shareholders. Just take a look at CEO compensation for these insurance giants and you will understand that profit is the primary motive of insurance companies. Thomas J. Wilson, CEO of Allstate, made $17,069,187 in total compensation in 2017. Allstate, in my opinion, is the worst of the worst when it comes to dirty insurance tactics and lowball settlement offers, but Allstate is not alone. Forbes notes that insurance executives make an average of $7.9 million annually.

How then do these insurance companies make all of this money? You guessed it...they drive up premiums for their insureds and they deny and minimize the amount that they have to pay in claims. I have seen dirty insurance tactics every day since I started exclusively representing injury victims

16 years ago. I have seen every trick in the book. So now, I am going to give you those tricks so that you will not fall prey to the insurance adjuster. You may not need a lawyer for your car accident case, but you definitely need to know the system. Here are the main things insurance companies do to shortchange clients:

1. **The Quick Settlement.** Do not take a quick settlement with the insurance company. This is a tactic to pay you as little money as possible without you knowing the full extent and nature of your injuries. It is also a tactic to stop you from hiring a personal injury lawyer to assist you with your case. Adjusters know that the involvement of a lawyer leads on average to a 3.5 times higher settlement amount.

2. **Signing Insurance Company Forms.** The insurance adjuster will try to get you to sign a lot of forms when you contact the insurance company. Beware of signing these forms. A medical authorization is always included in these packets. If you sign the medical authorization, you are giving the insurance company "carte blanche" to look into your past medical history. They will use these medical authorizations to gin up any type of excuse to claim you had a pre-existing condition that was the cause of your injuries. The insurance company may also try to sneak waivers or releases into the documents that they want you to sign. Read everything and assume nothing. Don't sign the forms!

3. **The Nice Adjuster Who Wants to Help.** Repeat this (silently to yourself) every time you speak with the adjuster: "The adjuster is not my friend." This is 100% true 100% of the time. The adjuster has two goals: to deny or minimize your claim. They are going to try to figure out ways that you were at fault for the accident. They are going to ask you how you are feeling in hopes that you will tell them you are "OK" or weren't hurt in the accident. They are going to be nice and tell you lies like, "We can just handle this together," or, "You don't need a lawyer." They may "accept liability" and then lowball you when you don't go see a lawyer or get the right medical treatment for your injuries. If you do one thing, be extremely suspicious of any insurance adjuster that tries to play nice with you. I am not giving you permission to be a jerk to the adjuster, just know their goals.

> *The adjuster IS NOT your friend!*

4. **Insurance Company Spying.** The insurance company will spy on you to claim that you are not injured in the accident. They may send private investigators to your house or business. If you are claiming a serious back injury, they may try to catch you outside doing yard work or lifting heavy objects. BEWARE, your social media is under attack. If you have a Facebook page, make it private. Don't talk about your injuries and the accident on social media. Be very careful about your posts and do not put anything on

social media that may be subject to interpretation (like a picture of you dancing at your cousin's wedding).

5. **Delay, Delay, Delay.** Adjuster's slow play is another trick used to frustrate injury victims. They may not return your call for a week, they may not return your call at all. The insurance company knows that you are probably in a tight financial bind after the accident, and they will use any excuse to delay your claim in the hopes that you will become frustrated and take their first lowball offer. They also may string you along by "accepting liability" and then lowball you when the time comes to settle.

6. **Requesting Too Much Information.** Delay's first cousin is the request for additional information. Adjusters will need you to get more information than is necessary to evaluate the claim. Once you send information, the insurance adjuster will ask you for some other piece of trivial information, and on and on and on. For this reason, I am only willing to provide (i) accident report; (ii) photos of vehicles and injuries; (iii) all medical records and bills related to the accident; and (iv) lost wage information, like a letter from an employer or copies of paystubs in a typical settlement demand. That is all an insurance adjuster usually needs to know to evaluate a claim.

7. **Recorded Statements:** You do not have to give a recorded statement or written statement (no forms!). I can count the number of times on one hand that I have let my

insured give a recorded statement to the insurance company of the at-fault driver. Even then, I made sure that the statement was later inadmissible. You don't have to give a recorded statement and it will most likely hurt you if you do. NOTE: If you are dealing with your own insurance company to get benefits after the accident, then you have a duty to cooperate, which may mean giving a statement or signing paperwork for your own insurance company.

8. **Copay Settlements:** Here is a nasty little insurance trick. The insurance company may try to settle with you by reimbursing you for the copay or co-insurance that you had out-of-pocket. Here's how it goes: the insurance company asks you if you have health insurance, then the adjuster tells you to go ahead and use that health insurance and she will give you a settlement to reimburse you for all of your out-of-pocket costs. Here are the problems with this scenario: number 1, the insurance company is on the hook for all of your medical bills, whether you have health insurance or not. The adjuster is attempting to severely diminish the value of your claim by offering to reimburse out-of-pocket expenses. Number 2, the adjuster didn't tell you that your health insurance company has a right of reimbursement for anything the at-fault driver's insurance pays to you. You may get a settlement of your out-of-pocket expenses and then turn around and be forced to give every penny of that money back to your health insurance company. The adjuster isn't going to tell you these facts.

9. **Disputing Medical Treatment.** This is a favorite tactic of the insurance company in pre-lawsuit negotiations and in litigation. An insurance adjuster with no medical training will nickel and dime the medical charges in an attempt to provide a lowball settlement offer. When caught, they will blame the "computer" that analyzed your medical treatment.

Your health insurance company has a right of reimbursement for anything the at-fault driver's insurance pays to you.

10. **Misrepresenting Insurance Policy Limits:** The insurance adjuster is not under an obligation to disclose its insured's insurance policy limits to you (unless you file a lawsuit, at which time they will be forced to do so). Especially if you are seriously injured in an accident, you need to know every source of insurance available. Beware when the insurance adjuster makes a policy limits settlement offer. You need to get a certified copy of that policy and an affidavit from their insured that he or she does not have any additional coverage. Let me give you an example. My firm represented two individuals who were seriously injured in a rear-end collision. The at-fault driver had a $500,000 individual policy that was offered to settle the claims. We filed a lawsuit, thinking that the at-fault driver (who was a wealthy businessman) had additional coverage. We were able to discover an additional policy of $10,000,000. Instead of the $500,000 offered, we ended

up settling the case for substantially more (millions) than the initial amount.

11. **Taking the First Offer.** The insurance company's first offer is almost certainly not their final offer. The only first offer I take is when the insurance company offers to pay their insured's insurance policy limits to settle a claim and I have verified the policy limits. For this, I recommend a lawyer. You probably aren't that experienced in negotiating on a day to day basis. We go to the grocery store and pay the price on the milk carton. Just know that this isn't the grocery store and negotiation is expected.

12. **Failing to Disclose Hospital Liens and Other Medical Liens:** The adjuster probably won't tell you that you may have to pay back a hospital lien or your health insurance company. They will offer you a global settlement. Then when you get the settlement check, you may be surprised to know that the hospital where you went to the ER is also listed on the check. When you settle, you have to make sure that all valid hospital liens and health insurance company liens and interests are satisfied. I could write an entire book on this topic alone. Negotiating these liens is among the top reasons you need to hire a lawyer (a good one that knows what they are doing) if you have a significant injury claim. It is incredibly complicated and you probably need a law degree to figure all of it out. But if you chose to ignore this advice, before you sign the release, at least ask the adjuster if they are on notice of

any liens to the settlement and how much. Then, call the hospital or health insurance company claiming a lien and try to work out a discount.

CHAPTER: 3

TOP 5 **WORST** AUTO INSURANCE COMPANIES IN NEW MEXICO

Here is my list of the Top 5 worst insurance companies to deal with in New Mexico. If you happen to be involved in a car accident and the other driver is insured by one of these 5 companies, please consider yourself warned! I am hopeful that the information in this book will give you a place to start regarding these insurance companies, but when dealing with the Top 5, we highly recommend hiring a lawyer. This information is my opinion based upon years of experience.

1. Allstate

There is no contest for who takes the #1 spot on the list of bad insurance companies. You are definitely not "In Good Hands" if you are dealing with Allstate. Allstate's handling of personal injury accident claims has led many injury lawyers, including myself, to conclude that they are at the bottom of the bottom of Santa's naughty list of insurance companies. A lump of coal is my Christmas gift to all of the Allstate executives and adjusters.

Allstate's reputation for being awful in the claims handling process is hard earned. Their claims handling policy has led the American Association for Justice (AAJ) to name Allstate as the "Worst Insurance Company in America" in its report The Ten Worst Insurance Companies in America.

They earn this reputation from a corporate culture instilled in them through a consulting firm, McKinsey & Co. In the mid-1990s, McKinsey was hired by Allstate to increase profits at Allstate. McKinsey's big idea was to lower the amount of money Allstate paid on claims, irrespective of the merits of those claims. Allstate took McKinsey's advice and made a conscious decision to reduce the amount it paid on claims. Allstate takes a "boxing gloves" strategy in the claims handling process. Allstate uses a one-two punch of lowball settlement offers and aggressive litigation. There are more complaints against Allstate than against almost all of its major competitors.

If you currently are an Allstate policyholder, my advice to you is to switch insurance companies immediately. We file lawsuits against Allstate insureds more than any other insurance company.

2. Progressive

Flo may save you "hundreds on car insurance," but you definitely won't "think easier with Progressive" when it comes to settling your car accident claim.

Progressive is one of the largest insurance companies in the United States. The company has been around since the 1930s and had revenues that exceeded $23 billion in 2016 according to their annual report to shareholders. If you are injured by a Progressive insured, get ready for a lengthy battle. In 2011, an Albuquerque jury exposed Progressive and its bad-faith settlement practices by awarding a man injured in a car crash $12 million against Progressive. According to an Albuquerque Journal article published on October 29, 2011, Progressive filed a lawsuit against an insured claiming reimbursement for two settlements it had paid to the insured following a car accident. Progressive claimed that the policies had terminated 90 minutes before the subject accident. The insured counter-sued for bad faith, and the jury awarded $11.7 million in punitive damages for bad faith insurance tactics.

In my experience, I generally see Progressive make unreasonably low first offers. After a lawsuit is filed, the claim is usually transferred to another adjuster who can, but not always, be more reasonable than the initial adjuster.

3. Fred Loya

Fred Loya is a Texas-based Hispanic 500 car insurance company and is #3 on my list of bad insurance companies in New

Mexico. Fred Loya is second in the nation for Latino business according to the El Paso Times. The company was founded in El Paso, Texas. Fred Loya is known for selling inexpensive liability insurance policies. Its agencies are often located in Walmart Superstores, Fiesta Marts and Big 8s.

In 2012, Fred Loya was fined $300,000 for violating state insurance laws after Texas insurance regulators found that the company used false advertising and did not give customers discounts as promised.

Fred Loya has a reputation in the legal community for being cheap when it comes to claims handling. I mainly see lowball first offers from Fred Loya. When the case goes into litigation, the case is generally handled by employee lawyers who have little incentive to advocate for their insureds. I frankly believe that when an insurance company like Fred Loya hires its own employee lawyers to handle claims, a conflict of interest arises. The employee lawyers are supposed to have a fiduciary duty to their clients, the at-fault drivers; however, these employee lawyers are conflicted because they are "captives" of the insurance company that employs them.

4. GEICO

GEICO the Gecko takes the #4 spot on my worst list. Geico is the third largest private passenger auto insurer in the United States. GEICO is also part of Warren Buffet's Berkshire Hathaway Group.

As reported by Business Wire (another Berkshire Hathaway Company), as recently as March of 2018, a

California jury found GEICO Insurance guilty of bad faith, breach of contract, intentional infliction of emotional distress and awarded almost $23 million in damages to a disabled Irvine man. The jury found that GEICO dragged out the man's settlement for almost six years and ignored requests to cover his medical payments and lost wages.

I have seen a change recently in the way GEICO handles car accident claims in New Mexico. We used to have an easier time settling claims with GEICO before filing a lawsuit. Now, it seems that it is much harder to settle our client's claims in the pre-litigation phase. The adjusters are trained to nickel and dime the medical treatment provided and allow meager amounts for pain and suffering. Because of these tactics, GEICO claims are some of the most difficult to resolve and oftentimes lead to a lawsuit.

5. State Farm

#5 on my worst list (and the 4th worst insurance company in America according to AAJ) is State Farm. State Farm is the biggest property casualty insurance company in America. Like Allstate, State Farm also utilized McKinsey and Co. to devise a way to increase profits by denying claims. According to the AAJ report, McKinsey devised a system known as the "three D's"—deny the claim, delay the payment, and then do anything to defend against a lawsuit. In its report, "The Ten Worst Insurance Companies in America," AAJ notes that State Farm "has gone to extreme lengths to avoid paying claims, including forging signatures on earthquake waivers after the deadly Northridge earthquake, and altering engineering reports regarding damage after Hurricane Katrina."

State Farm often utilizes teams to adjust claims. In my experience, this makes settlement of many State Farm claims a difficult proposition. Any one team member can work on the claim, but there is not one person assigned to an individual claim. For these reasons, there is one settlement authority assigned and no adjuster can offer anything more than the maximum settlement authority. This team-think approach makes settlement pre-litigation difficult. Without a primary adjuster to deal with, there is no discretion or incentive to seek higher settlement authority from a supervisor. Once a lawsuit is filed and a lawyer is assigned to the case, we are generally able to get a more favorable settlement for our clients.

CHAPTER: 4

DO I NEED TO HIRE A LAWYER FOR MY CAR ACCIDENT?

You may be asking, "Should I handle my own car accident case, or should I hire a lawyer?" Well, it depends. There are definitely times when you do not need to hire a lawyer to handle a car accident claim. You can generally handle your own car accident claim when the injuries are minor (subjective injuries that resolve quickly after the accident) or where there is only property damage involved. In fact, our law firm will not accept a case where the injuries are minor or there is little or no property damage. Most of the time, claims like these can be handled without hiring a lawyer. But still, if you choose to do your own claim, you should take the time to do some basic research before you battle against the insurance company. Read this book for great information to help you with your claim and to learn the dirty insurance tricks you need to look out for.

When and If You Should Call a Lawyer

Any time there are more serious injuries or death involved, a lawyer should be hired immediately. There are just too many considerations that you either aren't aware of or don't have the experience to handle. A good personal injury lawyer will have experience with thousands of car accident cases and will almost always put more money in your pocket than you could have received if you had tried to handle it on your own. If you or a loved one has been involved in a serious car accident, you should seek legal advice immediately. An experienced car accident lawyer will start investigating from day one. Because of the nature of the injuries and the stakes involved, it is imperative that you seek prompt legal advice. In high stakes car accidents, like those involving accidents with 18-wheelers, we will immediately begin gathering evidence, getting witness statements, hiring accident reconstruction experts, inspecting the vehicle, downloading the truck's ECM ("black box"), getting medical records and helping our clients receive needed medical care. Our law firm employs a rapid response team that will immediately begin gathering evidence that is crucial to a successful claim. If we believe you have a good case, we will travel to

ANY TIME there are more serious injuries or death involved, a lawyer should be hired IMMEDIATELY.

any city in New Mexico to meet with our injured clients or gather evidence.

Even if the injuries are not severe and you have what you consider a "small case," you should consider hiring a lawyer as soon as possible. Small accident cases frequently have to be litigated and tried to a jury. A jury will more likely believe that you are injured in the accident if there are not large gaps in time between the accident and the time that you wait to get medical treatment. The sooner you hire a lawyer, the sooner the lawyer can begin helping you get the medical attention that you need after an accident. As a general rule, our law firm will not agree to represent someone in a car accident if there are more than three weeks between the date of the accident and the time the person seeks medical treatment.

We know that sometimes people want to try and handle things on their own. That is why we are providing this guidance to you to help you deal with the insurance company, but we still firmly advise at least consulting with an attorney before you proceed.

Don't Screw Up Your Own Case

The following list provides guidance for those who want to handle a car accident case without the help of an attorney. Use these tips so that you won't fall prey to the insurance company tricks and tactics.

1. Don't Give a Recorded Statement

The insurance company will always try to get you to give a recorded statement. The adjuster will tell you that the claim cannot be settled until you have given a recorded statement. That is simply not true. We routinely advise our clients not to give a recorded statement. We settle cases every single week where no statements are given.

The insurance adjuster will try to take your statements out of context or will try to minimize your injuries in the statement. If the case ever goes to trial, "everything you say will be used against you." The recorded statement is a simple trick to allow the insurance company to minimize or deny your claim.

There are some instances when a recorded statement is necessary. For example, if the claim you are making is against your own insurance company for uninsured motorist benefits, you have a duty to cooperate. In those cases, we set up a recorded statement under controlled conditions and we prepare our clients to give all necessary information without prejudicing our client's case.

2. Don't Ask for Too Much or Too Little

The first mistake, asking for too little is easy to understand. If you ask for too little for your claim, you can realistically never go back and ask for more. The second error, asking for too much, is a little more complicated. If you ask for too much, the insurance company is going to respond in kind by offering very little to settle your claim. It may be very difficult to settle the case because of the wide disparity between the actual value of your claim and the demand you have made. In a car accident claim involving minor damages and little medical treatment that has resolved, I would suggest sending one global demand to settle your personal injury claim after you have completed your medical treatment. Add up all of your medical bills and lost wages, if any. Add to that number a few thousand dollars to compensate for pain and suffering. The more injured you are, the more money you can demand. If you have low medical bills and light treatment and then you turn around and demand tens of thousands or hundreds of thousands of dollars, you can expect to get stonewalled by the insurance company. Plus, you will communicate to the insurance company that you don't know what you are doing. Knowing how much to demand and why is one of the many benefits you will receive by hiring a personal injury lawyer.

3. Taking the Insurance Company's First/Final Offer

Another mistake we see is that unrepresented people take the first offer that the insurance company offers. You can expect that the insurance company will start with a low offer. Do not take it. The process is not unlike buying a product at a flea market. Assume that the insurance company has more money to offer you to settle your claim. Also, do not believe that the insurance company's "final offer" is really final. Oftentimes, you are able to get more money by demanding a number close to the insurance company's "final offer." Be willing to give the process time and to walk away from the deal if you do not believe that you are getting a fair offer to settle your injury claim.

4. Settling the Case Too Quickly

I hear the following all of the time when a new client comes in for a free consultation, "The insurance company offered to pay my medical bills and give me $500 for my pain and suffering." I always advise against this. Settling too fast is a trap for the unwary. Many times, your injuries may not be fully understood right after an accident. For example, let's say you're in a car accident and wake up with a sore back. You think it will just resolve on its own, but what happens if your sore back doesn't get any better after a few months? Then, you go and get an MRI which shows you have a herniated disc. This is a lot more serious than you first imagined. If you have already settled your claim, the insurance company does not have to ever give you another penny, even though you can prove that your herniated disc was caused by the accident. So, beware. The only reason the insurance company is offering you that fast settlement is to reduce the value of your potential claim.

Instead, you should wait until you have finished all of your medical treatment before you attempt a resolution of your claim. You should always know the exact nature and extent of your injuries before attempting settlement.

5. Not Knowing the Law

There is no such thing as a "simple" car wreck. In a car accident case, you need to know what laws will affect your claim. You should do your homework and research as much as you can about the laws surrounding car accidents. Take a look at our website at clarkharmonsonattorney.com which has a lot of useful information. Read the information in this book carefully. Research the New Mexico rules of the road found at New Mexico Statutes Annotated (NMSA) Chapter 66, Section 7. Know that your own insurance company may provide you benefits in addition to the at-fault driver's insurance, like Medical Payments Coverage and Uninsured or Underinsured Motorist Protection.

6. Putting Too Much Trust in the Insurance Company

People put too much trust in what the other driver's insurance company is telling them. For instance, the insurance company may admit fault for causing the accident in negotiations with you. Do not assume that the insurance company will live by that admission if the case cannot be settled. You should assume, despite what the insurance adjuster says, that the case is going to trial. You should investigate your own crash. Get a certified copy of the accident report. Speak with witnesses and get their phone numbers and

> *DO NOT give the insurance company a medical authorization.*

addresses in case you need them. Get a written statement from witnesses if available. Document everything. Take photos of your vehicle and the accident scene. If you can, get photos of the other driver's vehicle as well. Always order your own medical records. Do not give the insurance company a medical authorization. Giving a medical authorization will allow the insurance company unfettered access to your medical history. Only give the insurance company enough to document your injuries from the accident. Don't write a blank check to the insurance company by giving them a medical or other authorization.

Also, do not assume that the insurance company will be fair to you. An insurance company has two goals: (1) to deny your claim outright; or (2) to minimize the value of their claim. The "nice" adjuster that you have been speaking with gets a big bonus for denying or minimizing claims. The insurance company and its adjusters are not your friends. Do not take anything an insurance adjuster tells you at face value. Verify and research everything the insurance adjuster tells you.

7. Failing to Understand Medical Liens and Subrogation

My guess is that you have never heard the word "subrogation" before. I sure didn't before I went to law school. Did you know that buried deep in your health insurance documents, you have given BCBS, Aetna and others like them a right to recover a portion of your personal injury settlement? Did

Presbyterian or Molina Medicaid pay your medical bills? You have to pay a portion of your settlement to them as well.

Subrogation is a fancy legal term that means that your health insurance company (and Medicaid and Medicare and the VA and Tricare, etc.) has a right to be repaid when it paid for your medical care caused by a car accident and when you receive money in a car accident settlement from the at-fault party. You need to know that the money the at-fault driver's insurance pays you is subject to claims by your own health insurance or from the hospital if they have filed a hospital lien. If you do not take care of the subrogation interests and liens, you could be sued by your own insurance company or the hospital. An insurance adjuster is not going to bring these up in negotiations but will tell you about these rights once you have agreed to settlement terms. You might not know that the amount of money offered will be a whole lot less once the health insurance liens are satisfied. A good personal injury lawyer will know these laws and know how to reduce these liens and subrogation interests to the greatest extent possible.

8 Failing to Make a Claim Under Your Own Auto Insurance Policy – Medical Payments aka Med Pay

You may be entitled to make a claim for policy benefits from your own auto insurance for medical bills and lost wages. These policy provisions pay regardless of fault and whether or not you pursue a claim against the at-fault driver. In New Mexico, many insurance policies have Medical Payments coverage.

Medical Payments Coverage or "Med Pay" provides coverage regardless of fault in an accident. It is important to remember that Med Pay only covers medical bills. Lost wages are not covered under Med Pay. If you make a Med Pay claim, your auto insurance company will be entitled to be reimbursed when you get a settlement from the at-fault driver.

In addition to the above tips, you can review our official blog at www.clarkharmonsonattorney.com/blog/, which is chockful of useful information about the car accident process and the various types of car accident claims.

In summary, not every case requires an attorney. I hope we have pointed you in the right direction if you choose to do it alone. In cases involving serious injury or death or where someone does not want to take the time to understand the laws, it is best to hire a personal injury attorney to help you receive the most money possible for your injuries. Next, let's discuss how to select a good personal injury lawyer for your car accident case.

CHAPTER: 5

HOW TO CHOOSE **A QUALIFIED** PERSONAL INJURY ATTORNEY

Lawyer advertising is everywhere! I cannot drive down the street, watch a TV show, listen to the radio, scroll a website or my Facebook feed or do just about anything without a lawyer screaming in my ear that their firm is aggressive and that they will win the lottery for their clients. These ads promise the world. Unfortunately, a lot of injury victims end up at these "personal injury mills" where their case is relegated to an inexperienced attorney or worse, a non-lawyer paralegal. One lawyer in the city where I practice brags that he has represented over 20,000 people in his 20 years in practice. If you do the math (and believe this extraordinary claim), that lawyer would have had to sign up and represent 2.7 new people every day, 365 days a year (including Christmas) for

20 years. What kind of personal service are you going to get at a firm like that?

As you can guess, my advice is that you should not rely on lawyer advertising alone when you make your decision to hire a lawyer. It is often not helpful and can be downright false and misleading. Choosing a lawyer is perhaps the most important decision you will make in your car accident claim. A good lawyer can literally be the difference maker in the value of your case. With that in mind, here are tips that you can use when hiring a qualified personal injury lawyer.

1. **Do not hire a generalist.** The lawyer you choose should not "dabble" in personal injury law. The law is simply too complex and the claims process too intricate to be handled by a lawyer or firm that doesn't specialize in personal injury work. If you see an advertisement for anyone that advertises for Criminal Law, Immigration, Family and Personal Injury, you can bet that that lawyer is a "dabbler" who hasn't devoted his or her entire career to representing injury victims.

2. **Get a referral from a lawyer that you know and trust.** Do you already know a lawyer that you like and respect? Ask that lawyer for a referral. Lawyers know the system. They know who is good and who is bad. The lawyer's recommendation is important because their own reputation is at stake when they refer another lawyer. Our firm doesn't do real estate work, but my good attorney friend Steve Anderson sure does, and his work is excellent. Need

a criminal lawyer? Don't hire me, but I know who the best one in town is for your particular circumstance. Get the idea? Use your own lawyer's contact for help.

3. Research attorneys online. There is a lot to learn about a particular lawyer by reviewing the lawyer's website and other websites about the lawyer. Here are key attributes to look for in researching a particular lawyer:

    - **Experience.** As a rule of thumb, look for a lawyer that has at least 10 years of personal injury experience. It has been said that it takes 10,000 hours to perfect a craft. For personal injury lawyers, that well might be 20,000 hours. You need someone who has been there and done that. I worked for a mentor attorney for almost 10 years before I decided to hang my own shingle. That time helped me learn the ropes and the tricks and traps. I had time to experiment and make mistakes while having someone there to oversee my work.

    - **Significant Verdicts and Settlements.** Look at the website to check for significant verdicts and settlements of the lawyer. Verdicts and settlements aren't the only measures of success, but they're important. Ask the lawyer to provide a written list of representative cases that the lawyer has handled. Look for a lawyer that has personal injury trial experience.

- **Involvement, Recognition and Awards.** Check to determine the lawyer's community involvement in the personal injury arena. Is the lawyer a member of trial lawyer associations like the New Mexico Trial Lawyers Association and the American Association for Justice? Has the lawyer held leadership positions in lawyer organizations? Has the lawyer written on personal injury topics and spoken at continuing legal education? Does the lawyer attend specialized training in his or her area of law more than the required mandatory continuing legal education? Is the lawyer recognized by his or her peers?

- **Online reviews.** More and more people are looking at online reviews to help choose a personal injury lawyer. Read reviews on Google and third-party sites like AVVO or Yelp! to get a better feel for the lawyer and the type of service that you can expect. Endorsements from other lawyers are also important when looking at online attorney reviews.

- **Initial Consultation.** Ask for an initial consultation with the lawyer personally. If the lawyer is not the person at the first appointment, then you should think twice about the firm. Use your gut at the appointment. If the lawyer pressures you to sign their contingent fee agreement, be cautious. Most of our clients end up signing a contract with us on our first visit, but my answer is always an emphatic "yes" if the client wants to take the agreement home and think about it.

I hope the above list was helpful to you as you narrow down your search for a personal injury attorney. Now here is another list to help you decide which ATTORNEYS TO AVOID:

1. Avoid Runners at All Costs. Go running and screaming from anyone who calls you first. We call these people "runners." Running a case is unethical, illegal and can get you disbarred. In our city, a local "claims department" gets copies of accident reports and directs the person to an injury clinic. Then that injury clinic refers the victim to a shifty lawyer. How do I know this is true? I know because someone called my wife after a minor fender bender. The person on the other end told my wife she was from the "claims department" and told her that she had an appointment with the injury clinic. There are unscrupulous people like this in every city in this great state. Run! Run! Run!

2. Avoid the "Personal Injury Mill." Do you want to be a number in a TV advertisers' machine? I sure don't. How do you know if you have found a personal injury mill? When you call, ask for your initial consultation to be directly with the TV personality. Better yet, ask for the TV lawyer to give you a phone call back before the first appointment. When the TV star doesn't show up at the

appointment or give you a call back, know that your case is not going to be handled by the TV lawyer.

I also have a little secret to tell you—a lot of these TV lawyers are not well respected in the legal community. If you actually get a meeting with the TV lawyer, ask him or her how many cases he or she personally took to court last year. I know one prominent local TV lawyer who never goes to court. If he can't settle your case quickly, your case is referred to another lawyer to go to court. The lawyers the insurance company "knows mean business" haven't been inside of a courthouse in years. You won't always be taken care of by these injury mills. Isn't it better to go with a smaller personal injury law firm whose lawyers handle a select number of cases per year than a mill where you won't receive quality attention?

3. Avoid Out-of-State Lawyers. Your lawyer needs to be licensed in the state where your case will be filed. Several times a year, I get a call from a lawyer in California (or some other state) who has poached a Texas or New Mexico case. Here is how the conversation goes: "Hey, this is Mary from California. I signed this client a few years ago and I can't seem to get the case settled with the adjuster. Now I need a lawyer to take this case and file a lawsuit before the statute of limitations runs. I found you online." Then I say, "You should file it quickly." Then California Mary says, "I can't, I'm not licensed in New Mexico." Let me tell you, you do not want to be the client that California lawyer is talking about. I don't know

a thing about California law. That is why I don't accept cases in California. But I have studied and passed the bar exam in Texas and New Mexico. I know and study those laws and I use them every day in my practice. Please don't hire an out of state lawyer.

I hope this information helps you in your quest to find a qualified personal injury lawyer for your car accident claim. Now let's talk about all of the good things that a good personal injury lawyer will do to help you with your case.

CHAPTER: 6

WHAT YOU GET WHEN YOU HIRE **AN EXPERIENCED** CAR ACCIDENT **LAWYER**

Here is what you can expect to receive in return for hiring a qualified personal injury lawyer to represent you in your car accident claim. Remember that each case is different, and that not all of these tasks will be required in every case.

The steps and actions your lawyer will take are:

- An initial consultation to discuss the facts of the case, injuries and representation
- Educating the client on the personal injury claims process
- Investigating the facts of the case, including ordering a copy of the accident report
- Uncovering all sources of recovery, including the at-fault driver's insurance and the client's

- Communicating with fact witnesses and a police officer in order to determine liability
- Gathering photos of the scene of the accident and client injuries
- Hiring experts as needed, including private investigators and reconstructionists
- Fronting all expenses, including all court costs and expenses needed to prosecute your claim
- Helping with medical care, including referrals to specialists like orthopedic surgeons
- Helping with getting imaging studies done, like x-rays and MRIs when needed
- Analyzing all legal issues involved in the case
- Handling all communications with the insurance adjusters on all case related matters
- Preparing a settlement demand package to provide to the insurance company
- Negotiating a pre-lawsuit settlement when possible
- Advising the client on reasonableness of pre-lawsuit settlement offers
- Counseling client when and if a lawsuit should be filed
- Filing a lawsuit when necessary
- Sending the negligent driver a set of written questions and request for documents
- Responding, with the client's help, to questions and document requests from the defense
- Preparing for and taking the negligent driver's deposition under oath
- Preparing the client for his or her deposition

- Attending all pre-trial hearings and gathering all necessary evidence in admissible form
- Preparing and attending a pretrial mediation (settlement conference) with the client
- Preparing for and going to trial if settlement is not possible
- Appealing the case, if required
- Negotiating all valid medical liens

CHAPTER: 7

THE CAR ACCIDENT CLAIMS PROCESS

You may feel lost with worry about what to do after a car accident. You are no doubt in pain. Your vehicle needs repairs or is totally destroyed. An insurance adjuster is calling you repeatedly trying to get you to make a statement and you are not sure that you should agree. The hospital just sent you a bill for several thousand dollars in the mail. You don't know who to go to for help for your injuries. You are unsure if your health insurance is going to cover your medical bills, or, you might not have health insurance in the first place. Who is going to help you get through all of this? One or more of these concerns has prompted you to look into hiring a lawyer to help you deal with all of these issues. The following chapter explains what you can expect when you hire a qualified personal injury lawyer, and how much they can help you.

1 A No Cost Initial Consultation with a Qualified Personal Injury Lawyer

The first step is the initial consultation with a caring personal injury lawyer who will want to know more about you and the accident. You should not have to meet with an assistant at the appointment. At the appointment, all aspects of the accident should be discussed with the lawyer. The topics will include the facts of the accident to determine exactly how and why the accident happened. At the initial appointment, the lawyer will go over your injuries and the potential sources of recovery (including all sources of insurance that may be available to compensate you). The damages to your vehicle and property damages will be discussed. You should not be asked for money. If there is a good fit between you and lawyer, the lawyer will offer to represent you on a contingent fee basis. A good car accident lawyer will never ask you for money up-front and will not get any fees unless he or she is successful with your case.

After you have hired the lawyer, these are the steps that a good personal injury lawyer will take to help you with your car accident case:

2 Getting You the Right Medical Care

The most important consideration is to help you get medical attention and treatment for the injuries sustained in the accident. Our goal as injury lawyers is to make sure that you receive the best medical care possible, whether your injury is catastrophic or minor. If you do not have medical doctors and therapists, a good injury lawyer will work with affiliated physicians, facilities and therapists to get you all of the medical care that you may need after an accident. A good injury lawyer will work with orthopedic surgeons, physical therapists and sometimes chiropractors to get help for spinal injuries. There are other specialists like neurologists and neuropsychologists to help with traumatic brain injuries. A qualified personal injury lawyer will work with psychologists and counselors to get their client help with mental suffering after an accident, if needed. If necessary and appropriate, your lawyer can ensure that you get needed surgery and other inpatient care following an accident. The inability to pay for costly medical care should not be an impediment on getting the best medical care after an accident.

It is important that you let your injury lawyer know of any issues that arise during the course of treatment. If the treatment chosen is not helping or not helping as fast as expected, the lawyer needs to hear from you so that he or she can address any and all medical needs you may have. A good lawyer will also check in with you regularly to make sure that your treatment is going smoothly and helping to address any issues. The treatment course needs to be a joint effort of communication with the lawyer's office, you and your medical providers. Please call your lawyer with any

It is important that you let your injury lawyer know of any issues that arise during the course of treatment.

questions or concerns with your medical treatment. A good lawyer is there to help you.

3 Helping You with Your Damaged Vehicle

The lawyer will assist you in getting your vehicle repaired by the wrongdoer's insurance company. If your vehicle is beyond repair, then the insurance company will declare your vehicle a "total loss." If the vehicle is declared a total loss, then the insurance company must pay you the fair market value of the vehicle before the accident. If not a total loss, you are entitled to repairs and a rental during the reparation process. The process of completing the property damage claim takes a joint collaboration with the law firm, the insurance company and you. You can help by working with the adjuster to provide the location of the vehicle, taking the vehicle to the repair shop that is chosen, and coordinating the repairs with the body shop. The lawyer and staff can help by making sure that the process of repairs runs smoothly and by seeing if there are any issues with the repairs. If the car is a total loss, the lawyer can help you determine if the amount offered is fair to you. A good injury law firm will not charge any fee to assist personal injury clients with their property damage claim.

4 Establishing Liability of the At-fault Driver and Insurance Coverage

These are the steps that a good injury law firm will take to establish your claim. The lawyer and staff will obtain the accident report and review it to uncover any issues. The lawyer will undertake any investigation that is necessary to establish the other driver's fault. That might mean talking to witnesses, speaking directly with the responding officer, reviewing or taking photos of the accident scene, inspecting the vehicles involved and going to the scene of the accident to take measurements.

The lawyer will then send a letter to the at-fault party and their insurance company to notify them of the claim. The lawyer will also send a letter to your automobile insurance company to determine if there is any coverage that may help with your medical bills and lost wages, like PIP or Uninsured/Underinsured Motorist protection. The lawyer will then work with the insurance adjuster by telephone and other communication with the goal of having the insurance company for the at-fault driver admit that their insured driver was at-fault (for settlement negotiation purposes) and verify that the insurance policy is in effect and covers your damages.

5 Pre-Lawsuit Settlement Negotiations

If liability is accepted by the insurance company, the next step a good injury attorney will undertake is to attempt a pre-lawsuit resolution of your claim. The lawyer will not attempt to settle your claim unless and until you have either fully recovered from your injuries or have met maximum medical improvement. This is not a quick process. If the lawyer attempted to settle your case before you are done with your medical treatment, you might miss out on injuries that were uncovered during your treatment. The lawyer will not want to miss any item of damage that can be claimed for you in settlement negotiations. A quick settlement is almost always a bad settlement.

A question that we get asked many times during the process is, "What is the status of my case?" If the insurance company has accepted liability for the accident, then there is a period of time when you are getting medical treatment where communication with the insurance company is minimal.

There are sometimes when the lawyer might need to take immediate action to file a lawsuit on behalf of our injured clients. For example, a lawsuit might have to be filed promptly when there are issues with the statute of limitations or there are immediate needs to preserve evidence or address catastrophic injuries. But the typical case doesn't require the immediate need for a lawsuit. In New Mexico, there are generally three years from the date of the accident to file a lawsuit. It can be detrimental in some circumstances to file a lawsuit before you have reached maximum medical improvement because the court can make us deliver documents and evidence that has not fully been developed about your injuries or the accident.

Once your medical treatment is completed or the lawyer has a full picture of your medical damages and injuries, the lawyer will typically attempt to settle your case prior to the filing of a lawsuit. Sometimes a lawsuit is unavoidable, and a good lawyer is ready to file a lawsuit and take it to trial on your behalf if necessary. However, you might not need to go to court. Our experience tells us that you are oftentimes better off if you are able to settle your case before filing a lawsuit. A good accident lawyer will only settle your claim with your permission and if the lawyer believes the settlement offer is fair to you. A pre-lawsuit settlement will oftentimes be beneficial by bringing prompt closure of the claim and eliminating the inherent risk of a lawsuit.

These are the types of damages that the lawyer will include in our comprehensive pre-lawsuit demand package to the insurance company:

- All Reasonable Medical Bills (past and future)
- Lost Wages and Lost Ability to Earn Wages in the Future
- Loss of Household Services
- Pain and Suffering
- Mental Anguish
- Permanent Impairment
- Disfigurement

6 Filing a Lawsuit and Taking the Case to Trial

If your claim cannot be settled with the insurance company for the at-fault driver or the need otherwise arises to file a lawsuit without pre-lawsuit negotiations, the lawyer will promptly file a lawsuit on your behalf. Filing a lawsuit is an intensive and time-consuming process. It can take more than a year, and oftentimes longer, to finish the lawsuit process. These are the steps that will happen in your lawsuit:

- The lawsuit is filed and the defendant(s) have to respond.
- The parties in the lawsuit exchange written discovery like written questions called interrogatories and requests for

production of relevant documents. During this phase, you will have to meet with your lawyer and staff to answer questions and supply documents to the other side.

- Depositions take place. This is where you will have to go to a court reporter's office and give testimony under oath to the other lawyer. We will have the same opportunity to depose the at-fault driver, any witnesses and your medical providers.
- Mediation will take place after the above discovery takes place. Mediation is a court ordered settlement conference. A neutral person, called a mediator, will help both sides to attempt to settle the case before going to trial. The mediator chosen is an experienced lawyer or former judge that has extensive experience with personal injury lawsuits. This process is non-binding and confidential. Most but not all cases that are in the lawsuit phase settle at mediation.
- Trial takes place if the parties are not able to settle the case. The trial will be in front of a jury and both sides will try to win the case. A jury of 6 or 12 people will decide the issues of who is at fault and how much money to award for damages and injuries.
- Appeal. If there are significant legal issues in the case, you might need to have the case appealed to a higher court. This is a rare occurrence, but it can happen if there was some error or irregularity in the trial that needs to be ruled on by a higher court.

CHAPTER: 8

TOP 5 CAR ACCIDENT **QUESTIONS ANSWERED**

You no doubt have a lot of questions when it comes to your car accident case. To help answer these, I've listed the top 5 questions that I get asked at the initial consultation.

1. How will my car get fixed?

If another person causes the auto accident and that person has automobile insurance, the owner of the damaged vehicle is entitled to have the vehicle repaired by the wrongdoer's insurance company. If you choose to have your vehicle repaired by the wrongdoer's insurance company, there are a few things to keep in mind. First, you have the right to choose any shop for the repairs of that vehicle. The insurance company is not allowed to dictate where you take your vehicle to be repaired. Second, you have a right to choose the type of parts to be used in the repair. You are also entitled to a rental vehicle from the insurance company while the vehicle is being repaired. A good personal injury lawyer can help you get your vehicle repaired when you become a client. Our firm does not charge any fee to assist our personal injury clients with their property damage claim.

If your vehicle is beyond repair, then the insurance company will declare your vehicle a "total loss." If the vehicle is declared a total loss, then the insurance company must pay you the fair market value of the vehicle before the accident. Most people choose to let the insurance company keep the vehicle; however, you can choose to keep the totaled vehicle. If you choose this option, the insurance company will pay you the fair market value of the vehicle minus the money that the insurance company could have made if the vehicle was sold for scrap.

2. How am I going to pay for my medical bills?

If you are in a car accident, the person that caused the accident is legally required to pay for your reasonable medical expenses resulting from the accident. The problem that our clients often face is how to get immediate medical care during the process of working on your claim. Insurance companies will not pay your bills up front; rather, they will pay a lump sum at the end of the case to reimburse you for the medical bills you have gathered because of the car accident plus your pain and suffering. If an insurance company offers to pay medical bills up front and give you, for instance, $500.00 for pain and suffering, you should be very skeptical. This is a trick the insurance company uses to give you as little money for medical bills and pain and suffering as possible in the hopes that you won't hire an attorney. The insurance company is not looking out for your well-being in this instance; rather, they will try to limit the medical care that you receive, regardless of your injuries. The insurance companies know that once your attorney is involved, they are more likely going to have to pay a fair amount of compensation for all of your injuries and damages.

So, how does a good injury lawyer get you the best medical care available to address your injuries? The answer is that we have developed relationships with many providers in all types of medical specialties who will work with us to get you the best medical care available. Many of these healthcare providers will work on what is called a "letter of protection." A letter of protection is simply an agreement with a healthcare provider to pay for the medical care out of the proceeds of a settlement. These arrangements are legal in New Mexico.

We will also work with your health insurance company and with Medicaid and Medicare to assist with funding necessary medical care caused by the accident.

We will work with your health insurance company, Medicaid and Medicare to assist with funding necessary medical care caused by the accident.

Our #1 goal always is to restore your health completely or as close to completely as possible after the accident. We will work with the right medical providers to achieve this goal for you and to help ensure that the negligent driver and their insurance company pay for those bills.

3. How much is my case worth?

This is another question in our Top 5. It is a very good question because we all want to know what the bottom line is. The truthful answer is that when we initially meet with a client, there is no simple answer to this question. Be wary of an attorney that tells you otherwise or makes promises about how much money he or she can get you. What a good lawyer will guarantee is that the lawyer and staff will work their hardest to get you the absolute maximum amount of money for your case. We think of the "Three Ss" when determining the amount of money a case is worth.

- **Severity of the Injuries:** Simply put, the worse you are hurt, the more money your case will be worth.
- **Severity of Wrongdoing:** The worse the wrongdoer's conduct, the more money your case is worth. We are always on the lookout for bad conduct like DWI, or talking and texting while driving.
- **Severity of the Crash:** Generally speaking, the worse the collision, the more the case will be worth.

Another important and sometimes overlooked factor in determining the value of your case is the amount of automobile insurance available. A qualified injury lawyer will have the experience to discover all sources of potential recovery, including from the negligent driver's insurance and from your own insurance. The lawyer will work to ensure that all sources of insurance are available to compensate you for your injuries. In this way, we maximize the amount of money that you receive out of a settlement.

These are the elements of damages that the negligent driver is required to pay if he or she causes an accident:

- All Reasonable Medical Bills (past and future)
- Lost Wages and Lost Ability to Earn Wages in the Future
- Loss of Household Services
- Pain and Suffering
- Mental Anguish
- Permanent Impairment
- Disfigurement

A reasonable settlement offer should include all of your medical bills, lost wages and a significant sum for pain and suffering and your other harms and losses. At my firm, we will not accept a case unless we feel that we can get all of your bills covered and put a significant amount of money in your pocket after you pay for attorney's fees and case expenses. If an insurance company is not willing to fairly pay you for your loss, a good injury lawyer is ready, willing and able to take your case to trial.

4. How much is your fee?

At Harmonson Law Firm, we do not charge clients up-front fees. We only charge a fee if and when there is a settlement of your case or if we collect on a judgment after a lawsuit has been filed. If we are unable to get you money for your car accident, then there is no fee for our services. This type of arrangement is known as a contingent fee. A contingent fee shifts the risk of loss onto the attorney so that you do not have to worry about paying the lawyer on an hourly basis. Most, if not all, personal injury attorneys charge a contingent fee. An hourly fee would prove too costly for most injury victims. The firm also advances all case expenses. Those case expenses are then reimbursed to the firm if and when there is a successful settlement or collected judgment. At Harmonson Law Firm, we charge the following contingent fees:

- 35% if the car accident claim is settled before a lawsuit has to be filed
- 40% if there is a lawsuit filed but it is settled before trial
- 45% if there is a trial or an appeal of the case.

The increased fee is based on the fact that the longer the case goes on, the more time and money the firm has to spend on the case.

The fees that we charge are in keeping with the standard fees charged in the industry. The most important question you should be asking is not how much the fee is, but whether I have chosen the right attorney to represent me for my case. Choosing a law firm is probably the single most important decision you will make. Picking an inexperienced attorney or an attorney that does not have the financial ability to go the distance with the insurance company and their lawyers could mean the difference in a maximum money recovery and a mediocre recovery or worse.

5. How long will my case take?

This is a question that we get asked a lot. The only true answer, unfortunately, is that it depends. It depends on the complexity of the case, the nature and severity of your injuries, and the willingness of the wrongdoer and their insurance company to accept responsibility and to fairly pay for the damages, harms and losses they have caused to you or your loved ones. A quick settlement is almost always a bad settlement for the injured victim.

With that said, we understand the financial difficulties that a car accident can cause you and your family. That is why a good personal injury lawyer will work diligently to get as prompt a settlement for you as possible. At Harmonson Law Firm, we work diligently on each and every case. The first step we take together is to ensure that you or your loved one has the right medical treatment to address all of the injuries caused by the accident. Once you or your loved one has reached maximum medical improvement, then we communicate with our client and the insurance company to attempt a pre-lawsuit settlement of your claim. If that fails, then a lawsuit is promptly filed and a court date is set to allow a jury to determine the fault of the parties and the proper amount of compensation for your injuries, harms and losses.

While no case is typical, an average car accident case might reasonably take this long to complete:

- 5-8 months: minor injuries and the case is settled before a lawsuit has to be filed.
- 6-12 months: more serious injuries and the case is settled before a lawsuit is filed.
- 1-2 years: if a lawsuit is filed on your case because the insurance company contests liability or doesn't want to adequately pay for the damages. Also, if there is a catastrophic injury or loss of life involved and a lawsuit and/or trial is necessary.

CHAPTER: 9

WHAT YOU SHOULD DO **IMMEDIATELY** AFTER AN ACCIDENT

Every single day, hundreds of people in New Mexico are injured in car accidents. In 2018, according to the New Mexico Department of Transportation, there were 46,786 traffic crashes reported on public roadways in New Mexico. These crashes involved 116,020 people, with 19,790 people injured and 392 people killed. Here are some additional sobering statistics:

- A motor vehicle accident happens in New Mexico every 11 minutes
- A distracted driving crash occurs every 55 minutes
- A crash involving an 18-Wheeler or other large commercial vehicle occurs every 3 hours.

(2018 New Mexico Crash Highlights – New Mexico Department of Transportation)

While no one expects to get into a motor vehicle accident, there is a chance that you or a loved one will experience a motor vehicle accident at some point. It helps to be prepared in the event you are involved in an accident. The following is an overview of practical advice we offer to help you to know what to do after you have been involved in an accident.

1. Stop, Don't Leave the Scene of the Accident, and Make Sure Everyone is OK

If you are able to safely pull off the side of the road, do so. Check to see if anyone in the vehicle is injured. If there are injuries, the first call you should make is to 911. Provide the operator all relevant information, including your location or the nearest street address. The #1 concern in an accident is your health and safety and those of your passengers and others involved in the accident. Go to the hospital if you have or suspect that you have a significant injury. If you do not feel that you need to immediately go to the hospital, you should follow up with an urgent care facility or your primary care doctor as soon as possible following the accident.

2. Always Call the Police

You should always call the police in the event of an accident. We can't count the number of times a potential client contacts us and informs us that they agreed with the at-fault party to not call the police. "Let's just exchange insurance information" is what a driver who is at fault will try to tell you. Don't make that mistake. You should always call the police and attempt to get them to respond to the scene. A crash report from the responding police officer will corroborate your version of events as to how the accident happened and who was at fault for causing the accident.

When the police arrive, you should provide accurate and complete information. You should not admit fault in the accident even if you think you are at fault. Please be respectful to the police officers, even if the police officers are not being respectful to you. You will be given an accident information card and you will be able to receive a copy of the report a few days after the accident. Most accident reports are available online.

3. If the Police Won't Come, File a Report Under New Mexico Law

Sometimes, the police will refuse to investigate an accident if the vehicles are not significantly damaged and the persons involved in the accident do not have serious medical injuries that need immediate attention. Still, you should always call the police and try to get them to investigate no matter what. However, if they will not investigate, then you need to file your own report with the police.

4. Gather as Much Information as Possible

While you are waiting for the police to arrive, you should gather as much information as possible about the other driver. Get the driver's name, address, telephone number, driver's license number and insurance information. Take photos of the other driver's license and insurance card. If the other driver admits fault or makes any other admissions, make mental note of exactly what the driver said about the accident. Gather whatever information you can to help your case without being rude or disrespectful to the other driver.

Independent witnesses often make or break a car accident claim. If someone is nice enough to stop and act as a witness, please get that person's name, address and telephone number. Don't count on the police to record the names and numbers of your good witnesses.

Take photos and videos. Take photos of your vehicle and the other driver's vehicle. If you have cuts, bruises, or other injuries and are in shape to take photos, do so. Have a loved one take photos of you at the ER if you go to the hospital following the accident. Likewise, take videos to document the accident scene and your injuries.

Take detailed notes of the accident and your interactions with others. As soon as possible, write down all of your interactions with the driver and the police officer. Write down anything important that you can remember about the accident and your injuries.

If someone is nice enough to stop and act as a witness, PLEASE get that person's name, address and telephone number.

Gather all of your personal belongings before leaving the scene if you are able. Oftentimes, the car will be taken to another location by a wrecker and you will not have access to your vehicle for several days following an accident.

5. Contact Your Insurance Company

You should notify your insurance company shortly after the accident. Even if the at-fault driver's insurance will be responsible for your property damage and injuries, you should notify your insurance company. When you notify your insurance carrier, they will help investigate the accident for you. Even though you should contact your insurance company, don't allow them to take a recorded or written statement before you meet with an attorney to discuss the accident. There may be additional coverage available to help with your medical bills, like Personal Injury Protection, that can be triggered by notifying your insurance company.

6. Don't Give a Statement to the At-fault Driver's Insurance Company

You will most likely be contacted by the at-fault driver's insurance company shortly after the accident. The first thing you need to know is that the insurance company is not your friend. They have two goals. Goal #1 is to deny your claim in its entirety. If they can deny your claim, for instance, by blaming you for the accident, then they will do so. Goal #2 is to minimize the value of your claim if they can't accomplish Goal #1. So, you should never give any sort of written statement or recorded statement to the insurance company. You should assume in every conversation with the insurance company that they are working towards achieving their goals and not yours.

7. Contact a Personal Injury Attorney Promptly

If you are significantly injured in an accident, the first call you should make after your immediate medical needs are taken care of is to a qualified personal injury attorney. A good personal injury attorney can help you deal with the many issues that are going to arise after your car accident. A good personal injury attorney can help you get the medical help you need in order to recover from the accident. The lawyer can help you deal with the at-fault driver's insurance and act as an advocate for you to get the most money for your accident as possible. A good car accident lawyer will know answers to questions you may not even had considered, like dealing with medical liens and health insurance subrogation interests that arise as a result of the car accident.

CHAPTER: 10

THE RULES OF THE ROAD: HOW WE HOLD NEGLIGENT DRIVERS ACCOUNTABLE FOR THEIR ACTIONS

Receiving a driver's license is a privilege provided by the State of New Mexico. The New Mexico Department of Transportation, Traffic Safety Division (NMDOT) is responsible for enforcing the rules of the road, which often are common sense safety rules that are designed to protect all of us. When those safety rules are violated, the consequences can lead to serious injuries and death. The purpose of this chapter is to summarize the key rules of the road in New Mexico and describe the types of situations in which we have helped our clients enforce those safety rules.

Irresponsible and negligent people cause car crashes. At Harmonson Law Firm, we strive to avoid using the word "accident." Accidents happen. A car crash occurs because someone made the choice to violate the safety rules and endanger the public. When a driver's negligence causes another harm, that person is responsible for the damages, harms and losses occasioned by that harm. Negligence is a legal term and is defined as failing to do that which a person of ordinary prudence would have done under the same or similar circumstances. Negligence also means doing that which a person of ordinary prudence would not have done under the same or similar circumstances.

"Ordinary" means what everybody does—nothing unusual. "Ordinary care" means what a person being careful would do. It does not mean what a person not being careful would do. A person using ordinary care does not needlessly endanger the public. Remember, there is no such thing as care that needlessly endangers. As soon as anything needlessly endangers something, it is no longer care. Also, "ordinary" does not mean average. Average has nothing to do with it. If 95% of drivers speed on the freeway, that may be ordinary, but it is not ordinary care. "Ordinary care" means following the rules of the road, the safety rules that are designed to protect the motoring public. We use these definitions of negligence and ordinary care in everything we do, from communicating with insurance adjusters to fighting with defense lawyers and to educating juries who will ultimately decide your case if a settlement cannot be reached.

With that in mind, let's discuss some of the situations in which a person's negligence, a violation of the rules of the road, might cause a car crash and injuries or worse.

Rear-end Crashes

Rear-end car accidents are some of the most common car accidents. Failure to control speed and driver inattention are some of the most common citations that are given when a person causes a rear-end crash. Because rear-end car accidents are responsible for a majority of the car accidents that we handle, it is important for us to study the laws and safety rules that govern rear-end crashes.

What are the Safety Rules that Govern Rear-End Collisions?

NMSA Section 66-7-318-Following too closely provides, "The driver of a motor vehicle shall not follow another vehicle more closely than is reasonable and prudent, having due regard for the speed of such vehicles and the traffic upon and the condition of the highway."

What are Important Factors that Contribute to Rear-End Car Accidents?

The following factors determine the nature and severity of a rear-end car accident:

- **Vehicles Involved:** A vehicle's weight, size and shape may work to minimize or maximize damage in a rear-end crash.
- **Speed:** The greater the speed, the more likely an injury will result. With that said, injuries often occur in minor

"fender bender" accidents because of the force exerted on the other vehicle and occupants.

- **Location of Impact and Direction of Impact:** A straight-ahead blow generally will produce more damage than a glancing blow.
- **Head Restraint Location:** A properly placed headrest is the best protection in a rear-end collision.
- **Seat failure:** A seat failure during a rear-end collision may amplify the injuries and damages suffered.
- **Seat angle and back height:** For example, a headrest that is set too low may amplify whiplash injuries when the head rolls over the headrest. The optimal seat position is upright with the seat far away from the dashboard with safety belts attached and tight across the body.

Distracted Driving Crashes

Every day we are surrounded by drivers who are talking away on their cell phones, texting while driving or catching up on their Facebook feed. A lot of us understand that distracted driving is bad but fail to take a look in the mirror when it comes to distracted driving. We can handle it, we say, we are good multitaskers. We always keep one eye on the road while we text and drive. Does this sound like you? I am not proud to admit that I have held these views.

I have been guilty in the past. Like a lot of us, I was under the belief that I could handle using my phone and driving at the same time. However, when I looked at the statistics and saw the effects of phone usage firsthand through my representation of victims of distracted driving crashes, I came to the realization that distracted driving is devastating. My research has shown that distracted driving is just as bad, if not worse, than drunk driving. These statistics made me take the pledge to not drive distracted.

DISTRACTED DRIVING IS JUST AS BAD, IF NOT WORSE THAN DRUNK DRIVING.

We all know that distracted driving is dangerous, but just how dangerous is it?

Distracted Driving Death and Injury Statistic Summary

The following are the reported deaths and injuries caused by distracted driving reported in 2016:

- **Nation:** 3,450 Deaths and over 390,000 Serious Injuries in a recent year
- **New Mexico:** Driver Inattention is the top contributing factor in crashes (21 percent) and a distracted driving crash occurs every 55 minutes in New Mexico.

Distracted Driving Defined

Anything that diverts a driver's attention away from the road contributes to distracted driving. The most obvious and pervasive distracted driving risk is by operating a mobile device while driving, but there are numerous situations and objects inside a vehicle that can lead to distracted driving. Distracted driving occurs when a driver's attention is diverted away from driving by a secondary task that requires focusing on an object, event, or person not related to the driving task. Common scenarios that may lead to distracted driving include operating the radio, adjusting the air conditioning or heating, tending to a child, focusing on another passenger, applying makeup, eating or using a map or the car's navigation system. The new technology that comes standard in all vehicles like satellite radios, in-dash touchscreen computers and GPS systems can divert a driver's eyes off of the road as well.

How bad are people at driving while using their mobile phone?

A lot of people like to think that they are multi-tasking masters and that they are not impaired by checking that text message or answering that phone call. Research proves otherwise. Most people are not able to multi-task. Rather, most people are task-switchers and their minds are not able to focus on more than one task at a time. When additional tasks are added or tasks become more complex, switching takes longer, which causes task overload. Many psychologists have concluded from extensive research that when people task-switch, productivity is significantly reduced.

Even when a driver thinks she is "looking" at the road, she may not be "seeing" the road. Distracted driving takes the driver's mind off of the task at hand—operating the vehicle. Distracted drivers engage in "intentional blindness" because they fail to notice and respond to the visual cues. Someone driving while on a cell phone may see a road construction sign, but fail to process that he needs to stop because of intentional blindness.

When it comes to the ability to multi-task while driving, virtually everyone gets a failing grade. While driving 55 MPH, a car covers in excess of 80 feet every second. When a person sends a text or reads a message, the driver can take his eyes off the road for an average of 4.6 seconds. In that time, the driver will travel the length of a football field without any visual guidance. The overall crash risk increases 3.6 times when a driver uses his or her mobile phone while driving versus a person who engages in model driving (both hands on the wheel, eyes and ears on the road).

How many people drive distracted?

Distracted driving is a pervasive problem. Studies show that nearly one-third of all drivers between the ages of 16-64 read or send text or email messages while driving. Another study published in Proceedings of the National Academy of Sciences found that drivers of passenger vehicles are distracted more than 50% of the time. This distraction doubles the risk of crashing. According to the study, nearly 70% of the crashes the researchers analyzed involved some type of observable distraction.

Deaths and Injuries

Today, distracted driving is one of the most dangerous driving hazards and contributes to injuries and deaths every single day. The U.S. Department of Transportation's National Highway Traffic Safety Administration (NHTSA) recently released its Fatal Traffic Crash Data for 2018. In 2018, there were 2,841 or 7.8 percent of total fatalities in 2018. That equals almost 8 deaths every single day caused by driver distraction. In New Mexico, driver inattention was the number one contributing factor in all crashes (9,622), crashed involving injuries (2,926) and fatal crashes (29).

Why do these statistics matter?

We owe it to ourselves, to our families, to our passengers and to the motoring public not to drive distracted. I will be the first person to admit that I have texted or talked while driving. Maybe I was late to court and needed to send a quick email to my assistant. Maybe I was checking in at the house to see what we were having for dinner. It has dawned on me through my experience representing people who have been injured because of distracted driving that there is zero wiggle room when it comes to texting or talking while driving. Whatever the excuse, there is simply no reason that I, nor anyone else, should have been doing it. I have personally taken the pledge to not drive distracted. When I get in my car, I place the phone in the armrest compartment and don't take it out until I have arrived at my destination. Harmonson Law Firm is committed to doing our part by not engaging in distracted driving while on the job or otherwise. If you need me or anyone else from the firm while we are driving, we will call you or text you back when we safely arrive at our destination.

Has New Mexico adopted a texting while driving ban?

Yes. According to NMSA 66-7-374. Texting while driving, "A person shall not read or view a text message or manually type on a handheld mobile communication device for any purpose while driving a motor vehicle, except to summon medical or other emergency help or unless that device is an amateur radio and the driver holds a valid amateur radio operator license issued by the federal communications commission." The New Mexico fine is $25 for the first offense and $50 for subsequent offenses.

Drunk Driving Crashes

Here are some national, state and local statistics that illustrate the dangers of drunk driving:

- Drunk Driving is the NUMBER ONE cause of fatal car related deaths in the United States.
- Every 2 MINUTES someone in the United States is injured by a drunk driver.
- Every 51 MINUTES someone is killed by a drunk driver in the United States.
- 2 OUT OF EVERY 3 people will be impacted by a drunk driver crash in their lifetime.
- In 2018 in NEW MEXICO, 199 people were killed and at least 963 people were injured by drunk drivers.

What are the laws that apply to drunk driving crashes?

The New Mexico standard, also the national standard, for impairment which is a blood alcohol level of .08%. New Mexico also imposes stricter standards for drivers under the age of 21 (.02%) and adult drivers of commercial vehicles (.04%). Drivers can be compelled to take a breathalyzer and/or have their blood drawn in New Mexico.

How can you help the problem of drunk driving?

Our firm is proud to support MADD and we ask for your support as well. MADD (Mothers Against Drunk Driving) was founded in 1980 in California by a mother whose child was killed by a drunk driver. I first learned of MADD in my childhood in the early 1980s. The son of a family friend was killed by a drunk driver in my hometown of Lubbock, Texas. Because of this tragedy, the mother helped form the Lubbock Chapter of MADD. MADD volunteers were often seen at local schools, malls and community events displaying a mangled car that was involved in a drunk driving crash that took the life of a Lubbock teenager. The wrecked car was a stark reminder of the toll taken by drunk driving that has stayed with me to this day.

Since the founding of MADD in the 1980s, the number of deaths in the United States caused by drunk driving has been cut by 50 percent. MADD has helped save over 350,000 lives and counting by their efforts to end drunk driving. But, there is still a drunk driving epidemic. Drunk driving remains the primary cause of death on our roadways. Until there is no more drunk driving on our roadways, MADD will be at the forefront to end drunk driving. That is why we are proud to serve as a local sponsor of the MADD El Paso Chapter.

With over 350,000 lives saved and 820,000 victims served, funds raised through Walk Like MADD events allow MADD staff and volunteers to:

- Provide emotional support in the medical and legal problems that follow a drunk driving crash.
- Advocate for high visibility law enforcement.
- Push for interlock devices for drunk driving offenders (which have been passed in 30 states).
- Lobby for advanced vehicle technology such as breath or touch sensors.
- Provide public support like designated driver campaigns, public transportation and ride sharing apps.

Please consider supporting MADD in your area by donating your time or money or both. MADD is working to make a difference and stop the epidemic of drunk driving.

Passing on the Left – Head on Collisions

NMSA 66-7-310. Overtaking a vehicle on the left sets forth the standards for passing on the left.

The following rules shall govern the overtaking and passing of vehicles proceeding in the same direction, subject to those limitations, exceptions and special rules hereinafter stated:

A. the driver of a vehicle overtaking another vehicle proceeding in the same direction shall pass to the left thereof at a safe distance and shall not again drive to the right side of the roadway until safely clear of the overtaken vehicle; and

B. except when overtaking and passing on the right is permitted, the driver of an overtaken vehicle shall give way to the right in favor of the overtaking vehicle on audible signal and shall not increase the speed of his vehicle until completely passed by the overtaking vehicle.

While passing left of center, there is a high degree of danger because passing on the left can lead to a catastrophic head on collision. This exact scenario had fatal results to the husband of one of our clients on a two-lane country road on the outskirts of Anthony, New Mexico. An uninsured young male driver was weaving in and out of traffic as he passed car after car on the left of center. He misjudged the oncoming traffic and failed to yield to our client's husband who was driving in the opposite lane of traffic. The resulting collision seriously injured the teen driver and killed our client's husband. Because the husband was in a work truck, we were able to negotiate a very substantial sum because the company had a large UM/UIM (uninsured motorist) policy.

Red Light Violations

Red light violations also make up a large part of our practice and are a significant problem on our roads. Red light collisions can be difficult to prosecute because, on many occasions, the other driver will claim that he or she had a green light. We call these "he said, she said" wrecks. The plaintiff, the injured person, always has the burden of proof at trial to show that the other driver was at fault. At trial, this can lead to a swearing match between the injured party and the defendant driver. If it is just your word versus the word of the other driver, a jury may be more inclined to rule for the defendant because of the burden of proof. That is why it is so important in red light cases (and really any accident) to get the names and telephone numbers of witnesses to the accident. A good independent witness is better than your word, the defendant's word and the police officer's word.

Speeding

Speeding was a factor in 3,659 crashes in New Mexico, which accounts for 7.8% of all crashes. NMSA 66-7-301 sets forth the general speeding laws in New Mexico provides a duty to drive within the statutory speed limit.

Turning Crashes

Another type of case our firm handles with regularity are wrecks involving negligent turning. Typically, someone attempts to make a left-hand turn at an intersection or at another part of the roadway without yielding the right of way to oncoming traffic.

Entering Roadway from Private Drive

Another top injury case we handle occurs when a driver exits a private driveway and causes a crash with someone on the roadway.

Crashes with Negligently Maintained Vehicles

Every day accidents in New Mexico happen because of other drivers' negligent inspection and maintenance of their vehicles. These types of cases occur frequently with passenger vehicles. Even more problematic than this is when trucking companies and their drivers fail to inspect and maintain their 18-wheeler and other commercial vehicles. This can lead to catastrophic results.

Commercial Motor Vehicles: 18-wheelers

The federal laws that govern 18-wheelers and other commercial motor vehicles (like passenger buses and other heavy-duty trucks) and the companies that operate them are known as the Federal Motor Carrier Safety Regulations (FMCSRs). The primary purpose of the FMCSRs are to help keep us, the motoring public, safe from the inherent risk of 18-wheelers and other large trucks. Motor carriers that own and operate these large trucks are only allowed to operate on our roads if they agree to comply with the safety rules set forth in the FMCSRs. If an 80,000 lb. truck (the maximum weight limit of an 18-wheeler) gets into an accident with a 4,000 lb. passenger vehicle, the truck is going to win every single time.

These federal laws are therefore designed to help ensure that catastrophic injuries and death do not occur on our roadways. Even though we have these foundational safety rules, some companies and their drivers simply choose to ignore the rules. In an effort to maximize profits and keep their drivers and trucks on the road, many trucking companies simply ignore the inspection and maintenance rules set forth in the FMCSRs.

What are the main safety rules set forth in the FMCSRs that govern the inspection and maintenance of commercial vehicles like 18-Wheelers?

According to the FMCSR, found at 49 C.F.R. 393.3, trucking companies (known as motor carriers in the FMCSRs) must systematically inspect, repair, and maintain all motor vehicles subject to their control. There is no set interval in which the motor vehicles must be inspected because such intervals are fleet specific and are to be determined by the motor carrier. The term "systematic" means a regular or scheduled program to keep vehicles in a safe operating condition. A motor carrier is required to keep records for each motor vehicle under its control. The records must include (1) an identification of the vehicle; (2) a record of the nature and due date of the inspection and maintenance operations to be performed; (3) A record of inspection, repairs, and maintenance indicating their date and nature; and (4) a record of tests conducted on the emergency systems on the vehicle. The records must be retained for a period of one year and for six months after the motor vehicle leaves the motor carrier's control.

49 C.F.R. 393.7 prohibits unsafe operation of a motor vehicle and provides that a motor vehicle shall not be operated in such a condition as to likely cause an accident or a breakdown of the vehicle.

The trucking company and their drivers are required to inspect each vehicle every single day. Every motor carrier shall require its drivers to report, and every driver shall prepare a report in writing at the completion of each day's work of their inspection of the vehicle. The following is a list of the major vehicle components that must be maintained:

- Service brakes including trailer brake connections
- Parking brake
- Steering mechanism
- Tires
- Lighting devices and reflectors
- Horn
- Windshield wipers
- Rear vision mirrors
- Coupling devices
- Wheels and rims; and
- Emergency equipment.

Negligent maintenance and inspection of 18-wheelers is a major problem on our roadways, but just how bad is the problem?

Because 18-wheeler accidents often cause catastrophic injuries or death, our firm has formed a Rapid Response Team that will immediately travel to the scene of a serious commercial vehicle accident to gather crucial evidence. Our Rapid Response Team will perform a thorough investigation after a truck accident that results in serious injuries or fatalities. If you or a loved one has been seriously injured or killed in a truck accident, please seek help from a law firm with the experience and the money needed to pursue a truck accident investigation.

Other Rule Violations

Here is a non-exclusive list of other types of violations that occur on New Mexico roadways that lead to car crashes:

- Licensing Violations. Many drivers negligently operate vehicles on New Mexico roadways with no license or licenses that are suspended or revoked.
- Negligent Entrustment, i.e., loaning a vehicle to an incompetent or reckless driver.
- Duty to drive on the right side of the road.
- Duty not to pass on the right unless conditions permit safe passing.
- Duty to drive safely on improved shoulder.
- Duty to maintain a safe space between two vehicles.
- Duty to yield right of way when entering highway.

- Duty to operate vehicle in a reasonable and prudent manner under the conditions, for instance, duty to slow in rain and snow.
- Duty to not race aka reckless driving.

CHAPTER: 11

WHAT ARE THE MOST **COMMON TYPES OF INJURIES** IN A CAR ACCIDENT?

The following are the most common injuries that occur in car accidents. Your first concern after a crash is to fully recover or reach maximum medical improvement for your injuries. A good personal injury lawyer will help you get the right treatment for your injuries to get you back on track as soon as possible after the accident. Here is a list of the injuries we most commonly see:

1. Whiplash

Whiplash is a neck injury caused by forceful and sudden back-and-forth movement of the neck. It is called whiplash because the mechanism is similar to the rapid cracking of a whip. This motion can cause injury in the bones of the spine, the discs between the bones in the spine, and the ligaments, muscles, nerves and other neck tissues.

The symptoms of whiplash may include severe neck pain, tenderness, headaches (most often starting at the base of the skull), stiffness, fatigue, dizziness, soreness, decreased range of motion in the neck, pain and a tingling or numbness spreading into the arms.

Sources such as WebMD, the Mayo Clinic and my own experience show that whiplash injury victims may also experience blurred vision, tinnitus (ringing in the ears), sleep problems, irritability, difficulty with concentration, memory problems and depression.

2. Spinal Injuries

All areas of your spine may be injured in a rear-end car accident. Most injuries occur to the spine (like the lumbar spine (low back) and thoracic spine (mid back)) when the driver or passengers in the vehicle do not have time to brace for impact. This can occur when the occupant either is unaware of the impending collision or does not have time to react to brace for impact given that a collision can literally occur in less than one second. When a person is unable to brace for impact, the spine does not have a chance to stabilize and protect itself from the force of impact.

3. Head Injury

There is a significant transfer of energy in a crash which may cause the brain to twist in the skull. As a result, brain cells may be damaged or stretched in the accident from the unnatural twisting or jarring of the brain in the crash. A traumatic brain injury (TBI) may result. TBI is an injury to the brain caused by an external physical force. TBIs are not the result of degenerative (from the process of aging) or congenital (from birth) causes. TBI may cause a diminished or altered state of consciousness, which results in an impairment of cognitive abilities or physical functioning. TBI may be diagnosed with the use of imaging equipment such as computed tomography (CT) or Magnetic Resonance Imaging (MRI). Other standardized tests are useful to diagnose TBI such as an Acute Concussion Evaluation (ACE), Glasgow Coma Scale and neuropsychological evaluation.

4. Broken Bones or Ribcages

Broken or fractured bones are common car accident injuries. A person may suffer a broken rib or collarbone as a result of the sudden engagement of the seatbelt stopping mechanism. Broken bones, like arms, legs and ankles, may occur because of the body striking the inside of the vehicle.

5. Shoulder Injuries

The force of impact coupled with the sudden stopping movement of the seatbelt can often lead to shoulder injuries. Such injuries can include dislocation, torn rotator cuffs, labral injuries, SLAP injuries, Acromioclavicular Joint (AC Joint) problems, and bicep tendon injury.

6. Knee Injuries

Knee injuries often occur as a result of impact from the dashboard, steering column, or other objects in all types of car crashes. Common knee injuries may include:

- MCL Injury: The MCL (medial collateral ligament) – most commonly damaged ligament
- The PCL (posterior cruciate ligament)
- The ACL (anterior cruciate ligament)
- Knee sprain & strain
- Knee dislocation
- Knee fracture

7. Lacerations and Puncture Wounds

A car accident may cause glass to shatter and other objects to become projectiles. When that happens, lacerations and puncture wounds can occur. An airbag may also result in severe facial lacerations. A laceration is tearing of the skin (a cut) that results in an irregular wound. Lacerations may be caused by injury with a sharp object or by impact injury from a blunt object or force. Facial lacerations caused by shattered glass are the most common type of injury we encounter. Lacerations may result in the need for sutures or reconstructive surgery in the most significant cases. A laceration wound is often contaminated with bacteria and debris from whatever object caused the cut and may lead to infection. Because of this, it is important to get prompt medical treatment.

A puncture wound is a deep penetrating injury caused by a flying object striking a person in an accident. A puncture wound usually does not bleed excessively and may appear to close up. Puncture wounds are prone to infection and proper medical attention should be given to clean and treat the puncture wound.

8. Paralysis

Damage to the spinal cord after a car accident can cause severe nerve damage. Victims may experience reduced or loss of sensation or control over their legs, feet, arms or other body parts. In the most serious circumstances, spinal cord damage can lead to permanent paralysis.

CHAPTER: 12

HIT AND RUNS, UNINSURED MOTORISTS AND UNDERINSURED MOTORISTS

According to the Insurance Research Council, New Mexico has the 4th highest rate of uninsured motorists out of all of the 50 states. 21.6% of all drivers in New Mexico do not have any liability insurance even though it is required by the law. This can be very frustrating to someone injured by an uninsured driver. Fortunately, New Mexico has very strong uninsured motorist insurance protections that help protect victims involved in wrecks with uninsured or underinsured motorists. The following is a guide to answer some of the basic questions about the uninsured motorist laws in New Mexico.

What is UM/UIM?

Uninsured/Underinsured Motorist insurance sometimes called UM/UIM insurance is required in the State of New Mexico. Uninsured motorist protection applies if the at-fault driver has no liability insurance. Underinsured motorist protection applies if the at-fault driver does not have enough liability insurance to cover all of the damages suffered by the other driver(s). UM/UIM coverage provides for payment of property damage up to the UM/UIM property damage limits. UM/UIM bodily injury coverage provides for payment for medical bills and prescriptions, future medical bills, lost wages, pain and suffering and mental anguish up to the UM/UIM bodily injury policy limits.

New Mexico UM/UIM Statute

The UM/UIM statute is found at New Mexico Statute Annotated (NMSA) 66-5-301 and provides that UM/UIM coverage is mandatory in New Mexico. NMSA 66-5-215 provides that the minimum amount of coverage for bodily injury coverage is \$25,000 per person and \$50,000 per accident. The minimum amount of coverage for property damage is \$10,000 per accident. New Mexico allows insureds to buy more than the minimum limits of UM/UIM. We recommend that you buy as much UM/UIM insurance as you can afford given the high rate of uninsured motorists in New Mexico.

The UM/UIM bodily injury "per person" limit means that the insurance company only has to pay up to the per person limits for any one person involved in the accident. The "per accident" limit means that the insurance company is only required to pay the "per accident" limits no matter how many persons are in the accident. For example, if the minimum UM/UIM limits are in place, and there are 3 people involved in the accident, then any one person could potentially recover up to $25,000 but the 3 people together could only recover a total of $50,000 in the accident.

UM/UIM coverage in New Mexico is known as reduction coverage. What this means is that UM/UIM insurance will be credited for any liability insurance that is purchased by the at-fault driver and the UM/UIM driver's coverage will be reduced by the amount of the at-fault driver's liability coverage.

For instance, if a driver has no insurance, then there is no reduction of the UM/UIM policy. In that case, the UM/UIM insurer will be required to pay for all of their insured's damages up to the UM/UIM policy limits. If the at-fault driver purchased $25,000 in liability insurance, then the UM/UIM insurer will be reduced by $25,000. So, if the injured party has $100,000 in UM/UIM bodily injury coverage, then there is $75,000 in UM/UIM coverage as shown in the following examples:

$100,000 UM/UIM – $25,000 (credit for at-fault driver's liability policy) = $75,000 UM/UIM available.

$75,000 UM/UIM – $25,000 (credit for at-fault driver's liability policy) = $50,000 UM/UIM available.

$50,000 UM/UIM – $25,000 (credit for at-fault driver's liability policy) = $25,000 UM/UIM available.

$25,000 UM/UIM – $25,000 (credit for at-fault driver's liability policy) = $0 UM/UIM available.

Rejection of Coverage

Because UM/UIM is mandatory, New Mexico has very strict laws on rejection of coverage. In 2010, a pair of cases were decided that drastically limited the right of automobile insurance companies to allow insureds to reject UM/UIM coverage.

The first case is Jordan v. Allstate Insurance Co., 245 P.3d 1214 (N.M.2010). The New Mexico Supreme Court gave guidance on the requirements for valid offers and rejections of UM/UIM coverage. The court held that a rejection of UM/UIM coverage must be made in writing and must be made a part of the insurance policy that is delivered to the insured. In addition, automobile insurance companies must provide their insureds with the premium charges corresponding to each available option for UM/UIM coverage. If the insurer does not get a valid rejection, then the insurer must provide UM/UIM coverage equal to the liability policy limits.

In the second case, Progressive Northwestern Insurance Co. v. Weed Warrior Services, 245 P.3d 1209 (N.M.2010), the New Mexico Supreme Court required automobile insurance companies to offer UM/UIM coverage in an amount equal to the liability limits of the policy. Offering the insured a choice to purchase any lower coverage was the same as a rejection of that maximum amount of coverage. Therefore, the Court held that an insurance company cannot exclude the maximum level of UM/UIM coverage in an auto policy unless it has offered the maximum to the insured and the insured has rejected the coverage. For example, if an insured buys $100,000 in liability coverage, then the insurance company must offer the insured $100,000 in UM/UIM coverage.

New Mexico Allows Stacking of UM/UIM Insurance

New Mexico allows stacking of insurance coverage policies. Stacking simply means that the insured can combine the UM/UIM limits for the various vehicles that are on the policy. For instance, if you have three cars that premiums are paid on under the same insurance policy and you carry minimum policy limits of $25,000 UM/UIM on your three vehicles, then if you are involved in a car accident, there is $75,000 (3 vehicles x $25,000 = $75,000). As one can see, stacking significantly helps a person injured in a car accident because of the increased UM/UIM policy limits available.

Stacking applies to all of the named insureds on the policy. In New Mexico, stacking of UM/UIM is available on each policy in the household and all cars in the household. Stacking also applies to others depending on the relationship with the insured. New Mexico has created 2 classes of insureds known as Class 1 and Class 2 insured for purposes of determining stacking rules.

Class 1 insured include the named insured on the policy, spouse, and relatives of the insured that reside in the household. Class 1 insureds can stack all UM/UIM policies purchased by the named insured for all cars insured.

Class 2 insureds include all people that are present in the insured's vehicle at the time of the crash that aren't family or household relatives (for example, a friend riding in the insured's vehicle). Class 2 insureds can only recover the UM/UIM policy limits for the vehicle involved in the crash.

Medical Payments (Med Pay)

Med Pay provides coverage regardless of fault in an accident. It is important to remember that Med Pay only covers medical bills. Lost wages are not covered under Med Pay. Med Pay is offered in New Mexico but not mandatory.

CHAPTER: 13

ACCIDENTS INVOLVING 18-WHEELERS – A DEADLY PROBLEM

Imagine driving down the highway, eager to get to your son's soccer practice. You have a lot on your mind. You need to make preparations for your in-laws that will be staying with you during the week and you need to take the car down to the mechanic to have the car battery replaced. You are just about to exit the highway when you are sideswiped by an 18-wheeler. From this point on, your life has changed forever.

Stories like this are more common than you think. Just recently, critically acclaimed comedian Tracy Morgan was involved in a serious car accident in which the "30 Rock" comedian had to be airlifted after his limo was hit by a tractor-trailer. The tractor-trailer, which was operated by a Walmart employee, failed to observe the traffic signs on a busy New Jersey highway. The comedian suffered a broken femur, broken nose, several broken ribs and was in critical condition following the accident. Morgan ended up losing his best friend in the catastrophic crash.

It is clear that incidents like Tracy Morgan's require Congress to strengthen the laws on drivers operating large trucks on our public roads and highways to ensure that citizens are protected from serious harm. Despite the fact that truck, 18-wheeler, and trailer accidents are easily preventable, year after year, accidents occur around the country each day and family members of the victims are left to pick up the pieces.

Researcher William Harris suggests that the cause of most accidents is driver fatigue – working long hours with little to no sleep – as was the case with the Tracy Morgan accident. Despite the fact that the Walmart employee/truck driver had not slept in 24 hours, Walmart claimed that their driver was operating "within the federal hours of service regulations." In a recent article by the Huffington Post, it was also noted that the new 'rest rules' which Congress has implemented will allow truck drivers to stay on the roads for longer periods of time. This means that truck drivers will face little to no repercussion in vehicular accident cases if they simply follow federal bylaws.

With claims like these, it is no wonder that individuals feel that Congress is not doing enough to ensure that truck drivers are taking proper precautions.

Most truck accidents occur due to driver distractions (including inattention), driver error and driver fatigue. Truck drivers often drive for long hours at all times of the day and night and in conditions that expose them to fatigue. In addition, interstate truck accident data provided by the Bureau of Motor Carrier Safety of the U.S Department of Transportation indicate that driver fatigue is a major factor in single-vehicle accidents and rear-end accidents.

With the increasing need for trucks to transport goods from one place to another, odds are that many road-users will require representation for personal injury claims at some point in time.

Nationwide, there are 160,000 motor carrier companies that contract truck drivers to haul goods on any given interstate. A survey of interstate truck drivers in 1972 found that one out of every six truck drivers had at least one reportable accident involving personal injury or property damage. Although many truck accidents are caused by mechanical failure and road defects, most accidents are caused by truck driver error.

To provide you with a few numbers, The U.S Department of Transportation (DOT) released a report in 2014 that recorded an astounding 500,000 trucking accidents that occurred because truck drivers and large trailers (10,000+ lbs.) collided with other motorists or pedestrians. Out of these 500,000 accidents, 5,000 truck accidents resulted in a fatality. A 2012 Report by the National Highway Traffic Safety Administration (NHTSA) reported that 472 vehicles were involved in fatal accidents involving large trucks in New Mexico, 1,109 fatal accidents involving large trucks occurred in Arizona and 4,607 fatal accidents involving large trucks occurred in Texas.

Truck drivers should slow down in work zones, keep a suitable distance between other road users, be aware of their blind spots and drive defensively.

While the trucking industry is vital to New Mexico's economy and the overall economy of the United States, more needs to be done to reduce these increasing numbers. Opponents to Congress' current and lax legislation on truck drivers stress the need for stricter laws on the periods of time that truck drivers can be on the road. Further, there is a need for truck drivers, companies and trucking companies to ensure that their trucks are well maintained for all street conditions.

While all road users should do their part to maintain a safe environment for everyone, the onus is largely on the part of the truck driver to ensure that their large vehicles do not put pedestrians and other road users in harm's way.

If you or a loved one was injured or killed in an 18-wheeler accident, it is imperative that you call a personal injury attorney. The trucking companies and their insurers are very sophisticated. In any accident involving serious injuries or death, the insurance company will send a trucking industry defense lawyer to the scene of the crash if possible. How do I know? One of my friends, a defense lawyer at a local firm, is on permanent retainer by several trucking insurance companies. He routinely travels to accident scenes. His one job is to gather as much information and evidence as he can to deny or minimize the claim and protect the insurer and the trucking company. You need the same vigorous team on your side. I will personally travel to any city in New Mexico to meet with you and to employ a rapid response team to investigate the claim that will preserve favorable evidence for you.

CHAPTER: 14

CAR ACCIDENTS CAUSED BY EMPLOYEES IN WORK VEHICLES

We frequently run into situations where a person had an accident with someone who was on the job and in a work vehicle. While there are many similarities with a regular car accident, there are key differences that need to be addressed in order to help recover the most money for our injured client.

One of the key differences is insurance. In a typical car accident case, the other driver most likely has the minimum amount of liability insurance, which is $25,000 per person in New Mexico. In a typical work vehicle accident case, the insurance is much higher than the minimum limits. We have seen insurance limits as high as $1,000,000, sometimes even higher. In a major crash, the increased limits can help our injured client get necessary medical treatment and surgeries that may not be available in a typical car accident case.

In addition, in any lawsuit that we file involving an employee driving a work vehicle, we always sue the employer as well as the employee. An employer is liable for the conduct of its employee when the employee is working in the course and scope of his or her employment. This type of vicarious liability, known as respondeat superior, allows us to sue the employer and potentially access much deeper pockets than the employee. We have sued major publicly traded companies in order to get as much leverage as possible for our injured clients.

Employers could also be responsible for negligent hiring, training and supervision. If an employee has a bad driving record prior to employment, the employer should know of the bad driving record and not allow that driver to operate a company vehicle. We have also seen many situations where the employer failed to provide any training to its drivers on the rules of safe driving. This can lead to a lawsuit for negligent training of the driver.

There are many types of vehicles and situations where a company vehicle might cause an accident. Here are some examples of cases we have handled:

- A travelling salesperson for a multinational company violated the safe driving rules and crashed with our client in a rental car.
- A construction worker in a work truck failed to yield the right of way by exiting a private drive into oncoming traffic and injured our client.

- A dump truck driver did not pay attention to road conditions and crashed into the rear-end of our client's vehicle.
- An employee of a landscape company rammed his employer's pickup truck into the rear-end of our client's vehicle, necessitating our client's need for a neck surgery.
- A taxicab driver failed to follow the rules of the road and slammed into our client, causing neck and back injuries.
- A delivery driver for a local restaurant rear-ended our client, causing significant spinal injuries.
- An employee of a television production company ran a stop light and ran a production RV into our client's car, causing surgeries and other major medical treatment.

Another major type of work vehicle accident is those involving 18-wheeler tractor trailers. The federal laws that govern 18-wheelers and other commercial vehicles are called the Federal Motor Carrier Safety Regulations. If you are involved in an accident with an 18-wheeler, it is crucial that you hire a lawyer that is very familiar with the FMSCAs and has experience dealing with these types of cases. Federal law requires commercial vehicles to carry much more insurance than a personal liability insurance policy.

The driver of an 18-wheeler is called a "statutory employee" of the owner of the 18-wheeler. Thus, generally, the owner of the 18-wheeler is subject to liability and damages to the injured person regardless of whether the driver is an employee or an independent contractor of the owner of the rig. The FMSCAs have many regulations that are designed to protect the motoring public, including limits on the hours of service, driver qualifications, bans on the use of hand held mobile devices, driving in bad weather and many, many more. This chapter is not meant to delve into all of the requirements of the FMCSAs and tractor-trailer crashes; however, it is important to know that these types of accidents are not simple car accidents and there are many sources of potential recovery in these types of cases.

Our firm has handled just about every type of work company vehicle accident. We have handled catastrophic crashes that involve loss of life and life-altering injuries. We have also handled cases involving less severe injuries where treatment cured the injuries of our client. As a result of our experience, there are a few generalities that come to mind. In a major crash, the company's insurance will use all available resources to limit its insured's liability and minimize damages. Most of these cases require us to file a lawsuit and hire experts on the issue of liability and damages. On less severe accident cases, we have found that the insurance company will generally agree to pay more money to our injured client in order to avoid filing a lawsuit. While these are generalities, it is important to note that we have been able to settle major cases pre-lawsuit and we have had to file lawsuits on minor injury claims. Regardless, Harmonson Law Firm is dedicated to helping clients with major or minor injuries. You should not try to fight the insurance company and the company involved alone.

In summary, if you have been in an accident with the driver of a company vehicle, there are many avenues to explore, including finding out how much insurance is involved and discovering who to sue. Special rules apply to work vehicle accidents and you should hire a lawyer with experience to maximize the value of your claim.

In a major crash, the company's insurance will use all available resources to limit its insured's liability and minimize damages.

CHAPTER: 15

WRONGFUL DEATH AND SURVIVAL CLAIMS

In the most difficult cases, a loved one dies in a car accident that was someone else's fault. After the initial shock and denial have subsided, a measure of anger at the damage that has been caused by the at-fault driver sets in. You want the person that caused the accident to pay for their mistake. Your life has been turned upside down. There is both emotional and financial harm, but the greatest loss is the loss of companionship and society of the loved one; however, there are also very real financial losses that accompany the death of a loved one. How are you going to make ends meet now that you have lost the second income? How are you going to cope now that your loved one is gone? Is there anything that can be done?

The most difficult and heart-wrenching cases that we handle occur when we represent someone who has lost a husband or a child in an automobile accident. We would love to turn back time and make it all go away, but nothing can bring a loved one back. The only thing that we can do is to help the family receive as much compensation as possible to aid in the hardships and help a family seek closure by holding the guilty party accountable for their actions.

In this chapter, we will discuss the 'ins and outs' of the New Mexico wrongful death laws which are designed to compensate for the devastating loss of a loved one.

What are the New Mexico Wrongful Death Laws?

Under the common law (the judicially determined laws that govern negligence lawsuits), a person's right to recover for damages in a personal injury lawsuit ended when the person died. In other words, at common law, there is no such thing as a wrongful death lawsuit. To deal with that harsh reality, the New Mexico legislature enacted a statute to allow for recovery of wrongful death damages by certain family members. New Mexico wrongful death is covered by NMSA 41-2-1. The statute provides that a person is liable for damages because of an individual's death if the injury was caused by the person's or his agent's or servant's wrongful act, neglect, or default.

Who Can Recover for Wrongful Death?

There are only certain family members that can benefit from and bring an action for wrongful death in New Mexico. The surviving spouse, children and in certain circumstances, the parents and the siblings of the deceased may bring an action for wrongful death through the personal representative of the deceased loved one's estate. We call the class of family members who can recover "wrongful death beneficiaries."

What Types of Damages are Recoverable?

There are several types of damages that a wrongful death beneficiary can recover under the wrongful death statute. Recoverable damages include:

- Mental anguish: A wrongful death beneficiary may recover damages for their emotional pain, anguish and suffering that results from the death of a family member.
- Loss of Consortium: This is the loss of companionship and society occasioned by the wrongful death of a loved one.
- Financial losses: A person can recover for the monetary loss an individual may experience caused by the relative's wrongful death. These pecuniary losses may include loss of support and other financial expenses like living, travel, medical and funeral expenses.
- Loss of inheritance: This element of recovery compensates for the loss of inheritance the decedent would have accumulated and left to a wrongful death beneficiary if he or she had lived a normal expected lifetime.

What is a survival claim and how is it different from a wrongful death claim?

A survival claim is also allowed in New Mexico and it differs from a wrongful death claim in many important respects. A survival claim includes the claims of the decedent that accrued before his or her death as a result of the at-fault party's negligence.

The survival statute allows claims that a person could have brought during his or her lifetime to survive the person's death. Under a survival statute, a plaintiff representing the decedent's estate may recover any damages that the decedent could have recovered if he or she had lived. These include claims for medical expenses and pain and suffering experienced by your lost loved one.

! *If you or a loved one were involved in an accident with a government vehicle, time is of the essence given the strict notice requirements.*

CHAPTER: 16

WHAT TO DO IF YOU ARE INVOLVED IN AN ACCIDENT WITH A STATE, CITY OR COUNTY OWNED VEHICLE

If you are involved in an accident with a state, city, or county owned vehicle, a special set of rules applies. These types of claims are governed by the New Mexico Tort Claims Act (Act) found at NMSA 41-4. Generally, governmental entities and their employees working in the course and scope of their employment are immune from suit unless a special exception applies that allows claims to be brought. The Act provides specific exceptions to the general rule providing immunity. One exception occurs in a car accident (or an accident involving any other kind of motor vehicle, aircraft, or boat) caused by a government employee who was working in the course and scope of his or her governmental employment.

While the statute of limitations for most personal injury in New Mexico is 3 years from the date of the accident, claims under the Act must be brought within 2 years of the date of the accident. In addition, written notice must be provided to claims against local and municipal governments within 90 days after the date of the accident. Once the notice is provided, the injured person then has 2 years to bring the claim from the date of the accident.

Damages against the government are also limited under Act. Under the Act, the government's liability is capped as follows:

$200,000 for property damage, $300,000 for past and future medical bills, and $400,000 total to any one person for damages other than property damage and medical bills (for example pain and suffering, mental anguish and other non-economic damages). Further, the maximum amount government is required to pay to any one person may not exceed $750,000. Punitive damages are not allowed under the Act.

Claims against the federal government are governed by a completely different set of rules under the Federal Tort Claims Act which I will not detail here.

If you are involved in an accident with a government owned vehicle, it is crucial that you discuss your injury with a personal injury lawyer as soon as possible. These laws are too complex to handle on your own.

CHAPTER: 17

BICYCLE ACCIDENTS

An accident between a cyclist and a car or truck often leads to serious injuries. A cyclist obviously does not have the same safeguards as passengers in a vehicle. As a result, the bicycle accidents that we handle usually involve significant injuries which typically result in higher settlement values.

There is prejudice that needs to be overcome when it comes to representing bicycle accident victims, because some people simply do not believe that a bicycle enjoys the same rights and privileges as passenger vehicles. While the law is clear that bicycles have a right to be on the road, a good personal injury lawyer needs to beware of the prejudice and work to educate the insurance company, their adjusters and members of the jury about the law and cyclists' rights.

If you or someone you know was injured in a bicycling accident, here are answers to frequently asked questions that may affect your case:

What traffic laws apply to cyclists?

Bicycles generally have the same rights and are subject to the same rules of the road that apply to motor vehicles pursuant to NMSA 66-3-701.

Here are some other laws that apply to bicycles in New Mexico:

66-3-703. Riding on bicycles.

A. A person propelling a bicycle shall not ride other than upon or astride a permanent and regular seat attached thereto.

B. No bicycle shall be used to carry more persons at one time than the number for which it is designed and equipped.

66-3-704. Clinging to vehicles.

No person riding upon any bicycle, coaster, roller skates, sled or toy vehicle shall attach the same or himself to any vehicle upon a roadway.

66-3-705. Riding on roadways and bicycle paths.

A. Every person operating a bicycle upon a roadway shall ride as near to the right side of the roadway as practicable, exercising due care when passing a standing vehicle or one proceeding in the same direction.

B. Persons riding bicycles upon a roadway shall not ride more than two abreast except on paths or parts of roadways set aside for the exclusive use of bicycles.

C. Notwithstanding any provision of this section, no bicycle shall be operated on any roadway in a manner that would create a public safety hazard.

66-3-706. Carrying articles.

No person operating a bicycle shall carry any package, bundle or article which prevents the driver from keeping at least one hand upon the handlebar.

66-3-707. Lamps and other equipment on bicycles.

A. Every bicycle when in use at nighttime shall be equipped with a lamp on the front which shall emit a white light visible from a distance of at least five hundred feet to the front and with a red reflector on the rear of a type approved by the division which shall be visible from all distances from fifty feet to three hundred feet to the rear when directly in front of lawful upper beams of head lamps on a motor vehicle. A lamp emitting a red light visible from a distance of five hundred feet to the rear may be used in addition to the red reflector.

B. No person shall operate a bicycle unless it is equipped with a bell or other device capable of giving a signal.

C. Every bicycle shall be equipped with a brake which will enable the operator to make the brake wheels skid on dry, level, clean pavement.

Does Car Insurance cover a bicycle accident?

Generally, yes. The at-fault driver's insurance is responsible for your damages and injuries up to the driver's insurance policy limits. This includes your personal injuries and the property damage to your bicycle. Also, your own Uninsured/ Underinsured Motorist Protection (UM/UIM) and/or Personal Injury Protection (PIP) and/or Medical Payments (Med Pay) found in your automobile policy will apply while you are riding your bicycle.

! *A person who does not wear a helmet can still recover from the at-fault driver.*

CHAPTER: 18

MOTORCYCLE ACCIDENTS

Motorcycle riding is a mode of transportation that has peaked in popularity in the U.S. in recent years. According to the Motorcycle Industry Council, the total number of U.S. motorcycle registrations reached $8.4 million in 2014. The number of motorcycle registrations has almost doubled since 2000. Despite their popularity, it is far more dangerous to ride on a motorcycle than it is to travel by other means of transportation like a car or truck. A motorcycle accident can cause catastrophic injury or death. Below, I've listed some of the things you need to know when it comes to motorcycle accidents and the motorcycle claims process.

Motorcycle Accident Statistics

Here are motorcycle accident injury and fatality statistics in New Mexico for 2018:

- A motorcycle was involved in a crash every 8 hours
- 52 deaths, 840 injuries and 1,090 crashes involved a motorcycle
- 78.4 percent of all people on motorcycles in crashes were either injured or killed.

What are the New Mexico helmet laws?

All motorcyclists and their passengers are required, subject to the exception described below, to wear helmets that comply with the Federal Motor Vehicle Safety Standard No. 218. Such helmets will be equipped with a U.S. Department of Transportation-approved sticker. US-DOT approved helmets have a one-inch thick inner liner, a sturdy chin strap and weigh at least three pounds.

What are the most common causes of motorcycle accidents in New Mexico?

These are the most common causes of motorcycle accidents that are handled by our firm:

- Left turn accidents: The at-fault driver fails to see the motorcycle while turning left and causes an accident. Left turn cases comprise about 40% of fatal motorcycle accidents.

- Rear-end collisions: The at-fault driver fails to recognize the motorcycle and/or is distracted and rear-ends the motorcyclist.
- Side-swipe collisions: The at-fault driver attempts to change lanes and negligently knocks the motorcyclist off of the road.

What are safety precautions for motorcyclists and others?

Given the high likelihood of catastrophic injuries faced by motorcyclists, it is crucial that motorcyclists and the motoring public exercise due caution. Motorcyclists and passengers should always wear a helmet. Motorcyclists should not speed, as speed is a factor in roughly 1/3 of motorcycle fatalities. Motorcyclists should obey other traffic safety regulations, including driving one motorcycle per lane. Both motorcyclists and vehicles should leave a buffer between the motorcycle and the other vehicle. Further, obviously a person should never ride a motorcycle under the influence of alcohol. Did you know that more than 1/4 of all motorcyclists killed in traffic accidents were intoxicated at the time of the collision? I promise you that a good lawyer will not help you if you were blitzed at the time of your motorcycle accident.

Do I need a special license to drive a motorcycle?

Yes. On New Mexico highways, a driver must have a valid license with a motorcycle (W, Y or Z) endorsement to operate a motorcycle.

CHAPTER: 19

REPAIRING OR REPLACING
YOUR VEHICLE AFTER AN ACCIDENT

Let's face it, an auto accident is a huge hassle to deal with. Along with your injuries, you will be forced to deal with either repairing or replacing your vehicle, you will potentially be without your vehicle while it is being repaired, then you will be forced to deal with the insurance company to get the repairs, a rental car and/or the value of your vehicle if it is declared a total loss. It's definitely a headache, but it is something that must be dealt with in the auto accident claims process.

But all is not lost. There are a number of protections for the owner of the vehicle involved in a car accident. Let's take a look at what protection the law gives you as the owner of the vehicle.

Vehicle Repair

In New Mexico, if another person causes the auto accident, the owner of the vehicle is entitled to elect two methods of measuring the property damage loss. The owner can choose to either recover the difference in the fair market value of the car before and after the accident, or the reasonable cost of repairing the vehicle, if it is economically feasible to repair the vehicle. Most people in this situation choose to have their vehicle repaired by the wrongdoer's insurance company.

If you choose to have your vehicle repaired by the wrongdoer's insurance company, there are a few things to keep in mind. First, the vehicle owner has the right to choose any shop for the repairs of that vehicle. The insurance company is not allowed to dictate to you where you take your vehicle to be repaired. Second, the owner has a right to choose the type of parts to be used in the repair. However, the insurance company only has to pay a reasonable amount for the repairs and the vehicle parts.

On some occasions, it is best for the vehicle owner to use his or her own insurance to make vehicle repairs when they have purchased "full coverage." We counsel people to use this option when the negligent party's insurance is being unresponsive or the investigation of the accident is causing unreasonable delays and hardship on our client. If this option is chosen, you will have to pay a deductible for the repairs. Then your insurance company will be responsible for getting reimbursed from the negligent driver's insurance company for the repairs and for getting your deductible back to you. The technical term for this process is called subrogation. Another time when you should use your own insurance to recover for your repairs and property damage is when the driver who caused the accident does not have any insurance. In that circumstance, your uninsured motorist property damage protection should pay for your repairs.

Total Loss Damages

If it is not economically feasible to repair your vehicle, then the insurance company will declare your vehicle a "total loss." Another instance when the insurance company will declare a total loss occurs when the vehicle cannot be safely repaired. For instance, a vehicle is often declared a total loss when there is frame damage to the vehicle. If the vehicle is declared a total loss, then the insurance company must pay the owner of the vehicle the fair market value of the vehicle before the accident. Most people choose to let the insurance company keep the vehicle; however, the owner of the vehicle can choose to keep the totaled vehicle, which is called "owner retained." If the owner chooses this option, the insurance company will pay the owner the fair market value of the vehicle minus the money that the insurance company could have made if the vehicle was sold for scrap.

Loss of Use (Rental Damages)

The law allows the owner of a repairable vehicle damages for loss of use (rental charges) of the vehicle while it is being repaired. The owner is allowed to recover the reasonable rental value of the similar vehicle for the time reasonably required to make repairs to the vehicle. The owner doesn't have to actually rent a replacement vehicle to make a claim for loss of use. If the vehicle is a total loss, New Mexico law allows for a vehicle rental until a reasonable time has passed to allow the insurance company to make a settlement offer for the value of the vehicle.

CHAPTER: 20

HOSPITAL AND MEDICAL LIENS

You just were injured by another person in a car accident and were transported by the EMS to a local hospital. Several weeks later, you receive a letter from the hospital entitled "Notice of Hospital Lien." What are you to do? Does it mean that the hospital is going to file a lien on your property or house? Should you respond immediately to the hospital to pay the hospital bill? Why doesn't the hospital bill my insurance? What are my options? These are common questions that I receive from our car accident clients when they receive notice of a hospital lien.

The key thing you need to know is that the hospital or your health insurance company may be entitled to a portion of your personal injury settlement. Knowing what liens exist helps us determine how much money we are able to put in your pocket at the end of the day. One of my most important jobs as a personal injury lawyer is to negotiate with hospitals, health insurance companies, Medicaid and Medicare when a settlement has been proposed. I negotiate with the law on my side. This area of law is complex. Different laws apply to different medical liens and the amount of a discount varies based on the laws for each type of lien. Because of these complexities, I often get a lot of questions in this area. Here are answers to some of your most frequently asked questions.

How does the hospital lien work? I'm confused.

Hospital liens are governed by NMSA 48-8-1 through 48-8-7. A hospital lien gives the hospital the right to recover from the proceeds of an injured person's settlement or judgment. The hospital must meet the statutory requirements to validate or "perfect" their hospital lien which includes filing notice of lien with the county clerk and providing a copy to the patient (or attorney) by certified mail, among other requirements.

A good car accident attorney will help verify if the hospital's lien is valid. Also, we can negotiate with the hospital for a reduction taking into account attorney's fees, case expenses and the nature and extent of your injuries. It is important for you to know that the hospital, by filing a hospital lien,

---

! *The hospital lien only applies to money that you receive from the at-fault driver and his or her insurance.*

is attempting to compete with you for your settlement proceeds. Knowing every aspect of the hospital lien statute helps us either eliminate the lien altogether or to negotiate the best possible amount with the hospital.

Is the hospital filing a lien on my house or other property?

Fortunately, the answer is no. The hospital is not attempting to file a lien on your house or other property. A hospital lien does not give the hospital a lien on other property owned by you. By filing a hospital lien, the hospital is attempting to take all or a portion of your personal injury settlement. Knowing the law is the first step in either negotiating the hospital lien or having it declared invalid.

The hospital is trying to charge me an insane amount of money for a visit to the emergency room. Is there any way to fight the hospital's charges?

This is the most frequent question that we receive. Typically, a patient goes to the ER after an accident for a few hours and is discharged. Several weeks later, the client receives a very expensive bill from the hospital along with a notice of a hospital lien. We have seen a visit to the emergency room that lasted a few hours exceed $50,000. More commonly, we see hospital bills in the range of $5,000 to $20,000. The typical automobile insurance policy only covers per person losses up to $25,000, so a large hospital bill can eat up all or nearly all of a personal injury settlement. Is there anything that can be done?

There are some protections to fight the hospital lien. The hospital lien statute states that the lien only applies to "reasonable, usual and necessary hospital charges for treatment, care and maintenance of the injured party in the hospital."

If you receive a hospital lien notice, we promise you that the hospital will not send a bill with any sort of discount. You will receive the hospital's chargemaster rate, aka the "whole enchilada." The chargemaster, or CDM, rates will contain highly inflated prices at several times the cost of actual charges that the hospital could normally collect. If private insurance or Medicaid or Medicare were to pay for your hospital bill, the hospital would only be able to collect "pennies on the dollar" of the chargemaster rate. Why then should the hospital be able to collect such an exorbitant fee from you?

This is where a good personal injury lawyer can help negotiate the hospital lien and charges in order to put the most amount of money in your pocket from a settlement. If the hospital still will not lower or significantly reduce its lien, your lawyer should file a lawsuit for you. There are several types of claims that can be made against the hospital, including a claim that the hospital has filed a fraudulent lien or a declaratory judgment action asking the court to reduce the lien because the hospital's bill exceeds the reasonable and regular rate. Our firm has successfully sued for or negotiated many hospital liens on behalf of our injured clients.

What if my health insurance paid my medical bills? Do I have to pay the health insurance back?

Remember signing a bunch of forms when you signed up for your health insurance? Me neither. Well, even if you don't remember, you did. Deep in the agreement with your health insurance is a subrogation clause. Subrogation is a fancy legal word that means you have to pay your health insurance company back when you receive a settlement from the at-fault driver. How much depends on the type of health insurance you buy and the source of your recovery.

If you receive government benefits like Medicaid or Medicare, then Medicaid and Medicare have what we call a "super lien" on the settlement. These liens typically apply to all sources of recovery, whether you receive money from the at-fault driver or from your insurance (like UM/UIM or PIP). We deal with Medicare and Medicaid and are generally able to negotiate a discount.

If you have a health insurance policy that is governed by the federal law known as ERISA (large employers sometimes have ERISA plans), then the health insurance company has more rights to assert a lien on your settlement. One thing that we are able to ascertain is whether the health insurance plan is a "self-funded ERISA plan." If it is not, then the plan would be subject to our New Mexico state laws, which allow for a discount.

New Mexico has various equitable doctrines that allow for a reduction or forgiveness of subrogation rights under certain circumstances. Those doctrines include the made whole doctrine and the common fund doctrine. The important thing for you to remember is that if your insurance paid for your medical bills related to your injuries, you are going to have to pay or negotiate the health insurance subrogation rights. A good injury lawyer can help you maximize your recovery and reduce or eliminate the health insurance's subrogation interest in your settlement.

CHAPTER: 21

CASES WE **DO NOT** ACCEPT

Every year, we accept many car accident cases involving significant property damage and injuries. However, we do not accept every person's case. We are selective because we devote a significant amount of time and resources on each of our cases in order to provide the best representation possible. Described below are the types of car accident cases that we do not accept.

1. **Low impact collisions with minimal or no property damage**. If the damage to your car is minimal (bumps and scratches) we cannot accept your case. We do this because the laws and jury verdicts in New Mexico make these cases hard to win. My advice in these types of cases is to attempt to settle the case on your own or look for a

younger lawyer (with good credentials) willing to take on the case.

2. **Cases where the potential client's physical injuries are minimal.** We do not accept cases where the expected medical bills and lost wages are less than $2,500.

3. **Cases too close to the statute of limitations.** In New Mexico, a person generally has three years from the date of accident to file a lawsuit for personal injuries. My firm will not accept cases on the verge of the statute of limitations, generally within 6 months of the statute of limitations.

4. **Cases where the responding police officer(s) investigated and found you to be at fault for the accident.**

5. **Cases where the potential client has already hired another lawyer and is now looking to switch lawyers.** We have found through experience that this is a lose-lose-lose situation – for you, for us and for your other lawyer.

6. **Cases with significant pre-existing conditions in the same body part as that injured in the accident.**

7. **Cases where the potential client has been convicted of a felony or a crime involving theft or dishonesty in the last ten years.**

With that said, there are a lot of good clients and quality cases that we accept. We use our case selection criteria to help ensure the best possible service for the clients whose cases we do accept.

We use our case selection criteria to help ensure the best possible service for the clients whose cases we do accept.

CHAPTER: 22

RESULTS

Throughout the years of experience, we have been proud to help numerous injury victims and their families recover medically, emotionally and financially after some of the worst moments of their lives. If you aren't convinced of the help we can provide, here is a sample of some of the car, truck and motorcycle accident cases that we have handled for your review.

Please keep in mind that past results do not guarantee future success and the results obtained for every case depend on the facts of that case.

Rear-end Car Accident: $1,100,000

Clark represented an individual who was involved in a rear-end car accident. The client had to have multiple surgeries, including neck, knee and shoulder surgery.

Motorcycle Accident: $100,000

Harmonson Law Firm represented a man who sustained injuries to his back in a motorcycle accident when a driver failed to yield the right of way at a stop sign. Clark Harmonson was able to secure a settlement pre-litigation for his client.

18-Wheeler/Semi Tractor-Trailer and Bus Accident: Confidential Settlement

Clark Harmonson and the firm he previously worked for represented an Army sergeant when he was riding on a military bus to a field exercise. An 18-wheeler driver failed to yield to the right of way at a stop sign at a highway intersection and collided with the bus. When the bus driver was ejected, our client took the wheel of the bus and was able to safely stop the bus before it rolled over. Our client seriously injured his back and neck in the process. During the lawsuit, it was shown that the 18-wheeler driver negligently stopped at the marked stop sign. The case settled immediately prior to trial for a confidential sum.

RV Accident: $225,000

Harmonson Law Firm's client was t-boned after an RV ran a stop light in downtown. Our client received significant spinal injuries resulting in a micro-surgery on our client's low back.

18-Wheeler/Semi Tractor-Trailer Accident: Confidential Settlement

Clark represented two people who received significant spinal and bodily injuries when an 18-Wheeler rear-ended the vehicle occupied by the firm's clients on an Interstate in Arizona. The lawsuit alleged that the truck driver violated the Federal Motor Carrier Safety Hours of Service Regulations, that the truck driver was placed out of service prior to the accident and that the driver drove in unsafe weather conditions in violation of Federal Motor Carrier Safety Regulations. The lawsuit was filed in Texas and resulted in a confidential settlement for the victims of the collision.

Rear-end Car Accident: $1,102,500

Clark represented the passenger of a vehicle that was involved in a rear-end car accident with a Suburban.

Motorcycle Accident: $130,000

Harmonson Law Firm represented a man who sustained significant injuries in a motorcycle accident when a driver failed to yield the right of way at a stop sign.

Automobile Accident: $155,000

Harmonson Law Firm's client was a passenger in a single vehicle accident in New Mexico that resulted in significant injuries. Excessive speed contributed to the crash.

18-wheeler Wrongful Death: $295,000

Harmonson Law Firm represented one son of a man with five children who was killed in an 18-wheeler accident. The case was filed against the father's employer because of allegations that the father's co-employee was distracted and veered from the roadway, injuring himself and killing our client's father.

CHAPTER: 23

WHAT **OUR CLIENTS** HAVE TO SAY ABOUT US

"I have worked with several lawyers in the past, but having you guys represent me in this difficult time was great. You treated me with respect, not just like another case. I was able to communicate easily directly with you and not just have the front desk give me the runaround. It was direct and to the point, no playing around. Awesome job. I would recommend you without a doubt. Thank you for all your help. Keep up the good work for the people that really need it."

- Tony

"After my husband's motorcycle accident... we were both lost and wondering what to do next. When we met Clark, he explained everything from the beginning and kept us up to date of what the process will be and where we were at during the

process. Clark is an excellent lawyer and if I could recommend any lawyer for a personal injury case I have multiple cards of his in my wallet ready to pass out. He is very thorough, kind, and really cares! Clark is the best lawyer around, and we did our homework before meeting him. Clark came to our house due to my husband's condition and Clark also followed up at least 1-2 times per week checking on how we both were doing as well as keeping us posted of what will come. I thank Clark for coming into our lives, he is truly a heaven sent!"

-Angelic

"Mr. Harmonson was very helpful. I was able to call and speak with him right away in hopes to seek some kind of advice. He was very attentive and empathetic throughout our conversation. I appreciated mostly his urgency he displayed to simply just hear me out. He was 100% completely and professionally engaged the whole time!"

-ShinnelleRose

"Words can't even describe the amount of help the Harmonson team showed and their amazing customer service. Rosie was amazing to work with, not only that, very professional. He not only helped but he actually cares about his clients. I would and will always recommend Harmonson to everyone I know. They're no words to even express just how much I'm grateful for everything. Thank you!"

-Deseray

"I read a story where Clark handled a case similar to the one I felt I had. I contacted him and we spoke for a while and I came away feeling very comfortable with his firm. I then did some more research on the firm and I found them to be a perfect fit for handling my situation that could have been very embarrassing. Clark held my concerns in high regard and treated me and my family with compassion and caring yet he was very aggressive in getting me the compensation I deserved. Clark went above and beyond what I expected from him and he even has time to address any questions or concerns I may have even after my case was resolved. If I ever need an attorney, Clark Harmonson will always be my first choice. I highly recommend him because I know I can trust him with my life."

-A.M.

"Clark is stellar. Every step of the way he was patient and explained in great detail my options every step of the way. My case was incredibly complicated yet he put in 110% and ensured I understood all that was occurring throughout the process. 10/10 would recommend to anyone."

-Justin

"I thank the Texas Bar Association for putting me in touch with Clark! He demonstrated on a number of occasions his caring help! I was injured in Texas, but lived out of state. He would come to the airport and picked me up several times and made sure I was taken care of every step of the way! I had to return and Clark was always there with a smile and stability that I needed! Thank you Clark for you and your wife's support!!!"

-Gregory

"My wife and I were in a car accident last year. We reached out to Mr. Harmonson he got right on our cases. Everything went smooth he kept our family informed of everything. He went above and beyond for our family. I would recommend this personal injury attorney for everyone. Exceptional and very great service."

-Quenton

"Mr. Harmonson was very professional and compassionate in the representation of my case. I can definitely say he is reliable and trustworthy. I was never left wondering where anything stood. I thank him from the bottom of my heart."

-Carlos

"Clark has represented me on two separate occasions and both times I've come out with a smile on my face. He and his staff are very professional yet friendly and courteous. They answer all your questions and will respond to you quickly. I felt comfortable and never uneasy like some people do when they speak with attorneys. I recommend him to all my coworkers who may need representation and if the need ever arises again you can bet your bottom dollar I'll be calling Clark once again."

-Mario

CHAPTER: 24

ABOUT THE AUTHOR

When Clark was twelve years old, inspired by watching the legal thriller *Jagged Edge*, he penned a note to his mom that said he "was going to be the best criminal defense lawyer in history." Clark's mom still has that note some 30+ years later. Although that dream didn't become a reality in the strictest sense, Clark stayed true to his commitment and became a lawyer fighting for justice. Clark has devoted his practice to seeking justice for clients that have been treated unfairly by the system, namely the insurance industry and their armies of adjusters and lawyers.

For more than 16 years, Clark Harmonson has devoted his life to helping injury victims, acting as a lighthouse for people who are lost in the sea of confusion that surrounds the personal injury claims process. He has routinely taken on major insurance companies on behalf of his injured clients, fighting for the fair compensation and justice his clients are owed.

Clark understands that facing an unexpected, life-altering injury is difficult enough—dealing with insurance companies that are determined to devalue or deny your claim can be outright overwhelming. Clark has the extensive experience, skills, and resources needed to battle with insurance companies so that you don't have to. With every case he takes on, Clark strives to recover the maximum compensation his clients deserve so that the client can focus on getting needed medical care and treatment.

Clark Harmonson

- Since 2004, has fought insurance companies exclusively
- Listed in Texas Super Lawyers – Rising Stars 2012-2014, a service of Thomson Reuters
- Sustaining Member of New Mexico Trial Lawyers Association and American Association for Justice
- Member and Past President of El Paso Trial Lawyers Association
- Written several articles for lawyers about personal injury claims

- Graduated summa cum laude (highest honors) and 2nd in his class

Clark Harmonson has deep West Texas roots. He grew up in Lubbock where he went to Monterey High School and Texas Tech University. He went to South Texas College of Law in Houston, Texas and graduated with highest honors (summa cum laude) and 2nd in his class. His law school classmates voted him Most Outstanding Male Graduate. After a brief stay at a major international law firm, Clark went back to his West Texas roots and moved to El Paso.

Clark loves his adopted hometown of El Paso, its culture, its people and its food! Clark serves on the board of directors of the Rotary Club of El Paso, a service organization committed to making El Paso and the surrounding community an outstanding place to live. Clark and his family are members of St. Francis Anglican Church. Clark serves on the vestry and as a legal advisor to St. Francis and the Diocese of CANA West.

Clark also loves New Mexico. Clark has travelled the world, but he would trade all of it for a good plate of red enchiladas from Chope's in La Mesa or a good hike in Taos or Santa Fe. Clark has been licensed in New Mexico since 2007 and has been involved in many high-profile cases in New Mexico. He has an office in downtown Las Cruces and has litigated cases all over the state.

Clark loves running and recently completed his eleventh half marathon or marathon. You can usually find him somewhere in the middle of the pack because Clark also loves eating tacos (his favorite in the world being from El Parasol in Santa Fe). Clark is married to the love of his life Sheri, who also happens to be his boss. Sheri doubles as the office manager at Harmonson Law Firm. Clark and Sheri have three kids. Their two children Clayton and Claire are 15 and 12 years old, and keep a watchful eye on their little brother Winn who blessed the family in late 2018.

HARMONSON
LAW FIRM
KEEPING YOU FIRST

WA

Made in the USA
Monee, IL
04 November 2026

67381824R10089